CYCLING HAWAII

Jeff Baldwin

BICYCLE BOOKS

FROM

Motorbooks International

Publishers & Wholesalers ®

First published in 1997 by Motorbooks International Publishers & Wholesalers, 729 Prospect Avenue, PO Box 1, Osceola, WI 54020 USA

Library of Congress Cataloging-in-Publication Data
Baldwin, Jeff.
        Cycling Hawaii/Jeff Baldwin.
        p.cm.—(Bicycle books)
        Includes index.
        ISBN 0-933201-85-0 (pbk.: alk. paper)
        1. Cycling—Hawaii—Guidebooks. I. Title. II. Series.
GV1045.5.H3B35   1997
919.6904'41—dc21 97-38895

Printed in the United States of America

Contents

About the Author

Jeff Baldwin is currently a Graduate student of Geography at the University of Oregon. After graduating with a Finance degree in 1979 he pursued a career as a fine art photographer for 12 years culminating with a solo show at 55 Mercer Gallery in Manhattan. He plans to combine future touring with his geographic studies.

Acknowledgments

This book would not have been possible without the information and services available through the University of Oregon. Specifically I express gratitude to the Map Library within the Geography Department for providing access to an extensive collection of base map materials. Thanks also to the Social Science Instructional Learning Lab and its fine staff for helping me through the trials of learning a complex computer graphics program for the production of the maps. Finally, to Bill Loy, professor of Cartography, who taught me about making maps.

Composing a book of this nature is a long term, time consuming process. Through it all my family, both blood and kindred spirits, have provided encouragement and support of the project, and forbearance of my absence, both emotional and corporeal. Thanks especially to my folks Bob and Dana, and my family, Laura and Carole.

Chapter 1

Cycling Hawaii

Why Cycle Tour Hawaii?

To cycle Hawaii you experience a place and its people with an intimacy unattainable from a car. From your bike saddle you will smell the African tulip trees, you will hear the rustle of giant ginger plants stirred by roadside waterfalls, you will see island wildlife normally scared off by cars, and you will feel the cool spray of surf breaking on cobbled beaches.

To the natives, you stand apart from the crush of tourists having a "fast" vacation. People express an interest in you and your journey and often offer assistance ranging from well wishes to invitations to free accommodations. People are proud of their homelands and see cyclists as people who care enough about their place to take the time to get to know them.

Legend

—————— Major Roadway

—————— Other paved roads

.... Unpaved roads and trails

Specified route

Alternative route

Area of map

  Beach

Airport

Grocery market

Λ Camping area

Hawaii offers the cyclist a tremendous variety of landscape and challenge. You can circumnavigate all of Oahu on a beach hugging highway and never climb above 300 feet. On Lana'i there are several days worth of challenging dirt road riding where you can feel as though you are the only person for miles. On Maui you can climb to the 10,000-foot summit of the Haleakala on a well paved, expertly graded highway, and then glide back down to the warm sea.

Perhaps the most obvious reason to tour in Hawaii is that no matter how the weather is where you are, the weather in Hawaii is almost always better: warm, gentle, and sunny. Imagine how much easier your winters would be if you spent a week or two in January pedaling from beach to beach in tropical sunshine.

It's been said that an "adventure" is an experience that is more enjoyable to tell about than to live through. This book can guide you throughout

Hawaii, and help you avoid the unpleasant "adventures" so frustrating to the first-time visitor. The travel log informs you of opportunities and warns against perils. The maps will make it easy for you to find yourself on the route of your choice, and the route profiles help you determine the difficulty of each route for yourself.

One of the best reasons for cycling Hawaii is affordability. On my most recent tour I spent an average of $12 per day. By cycling you avoid the cost of a rental car. By camping you avoid the cost of resort hotels which begin at $55 and go up from there. At Manele Bay on Lana'i, for example, you can pay $5 a night to camp on a shady lawn 100 feet from a splendid beach frequented by dolphin, or you can rent a room starting at $225 at the resort which is over 1,000 feet from the same beach. Campground fees range from the free sites in both the Haleakala National Park and many State and County Parks to the high of the $10 fee charged at Camp Pecosa on Maui. By cooking your own food you not only get to control what's going into your body but, again, you save on the cost of eating every meal at a restaurant.

Hawaii is waiting for you; why wait any longer?

Getting There

Although there are ships that visit Hawaii from the Mainland, air travel is the only practical way to reach these most isolated of Pacific islands. The Sunday Travel section in your local, large urban newspaper probably lists the cheapest published fare to Hawaii from that city. Use this figure as a benchmark. Call the identified airline to confirm that the listed price is valid for the period in which you want to travel, then call a few travel agents to seek a better deal. Agents have access to charters and packages that we mere mortals do not.

Remember that you can access the free "800" numbers for the airlines any time of the day or night. Call Toll Free Information at 1-800-555-1212 and ask for the number of the desired carrier. Hawaiian, United, Northwest, American, and Delta are among the major airlines offering regular service.

Many airlines now alternate Hawaiian destinations between Kahului, Maui, and Honolulu on Oahu. Your desired destination may, therefore, dictate what day you leave home and what day you return. Interisland flights are plentiful if the trans-Pacific schedules don't fit your itinerary.

Getting Around

There are a variety of options with regard to non-bike travel on the islands. There are always taxis. Many hotels and communities provide shuttles to and from the airport. Oahu has an outstanding public bus system. Where-ever practical, I've included specifics in the introductory chapters for each island.

With the exception of congested Honolulu, riding your bike to and from the airport is easy and pleasant.

Visas

Hawaii is a member State of the United States. Regulations governing visitation by foreign nationals, therefore, are the same for Hawaii as for the rest of the United States. Canadians do not need either visas or passports; however, some form of official identification such as passport, driver's license, or birth certificate is required. Most other nationalities must meet passport, visa, and minimum cash holding requirements to enter Hawaii. You can ask your travel agent or the nearest U.S. consulate in your country for details.

Environmental Conditions

The weather in and around Maui County is extremely varied. On any given day there may be frost or even snow on top of the Haleakala, warm winds and showers over central Moloka'i, and near-drought conditions on the west side of Lana'i, all at the same time.

Generally, the temperature near sea level on all of the islands swings daily around the temperature of the ocean. June through September sees daytime highs near 90 degrees and evening lows near 68 degrees. Winter temperatures are slightly lower, with highs near 78 degrees and lows around 60 degrees. Obviously, a large portion of the islands' area is above sea level and the temperature in these areas become cooler with increased elevation. As a rule, the temperature will decrease 3.5 degrees for every 1,000-foot increase in elevation so that a balmy 68-degree night in Ka'anapali translates into a 44-degree chill at Hosmer Grove Campground two-thirds of the way up the Haleakala, and 33 degrees at the 10,300-foot summit.

Humidity also varies markedly around the islands. Maui is generally more humid than Moloka'i, and Lana'i feels generally desert-like in its comparative dryness. The eastern windward sides of the islands are more humid than the western leeward sides. Humidity also decreases markedly with elevation so that Kula in the Maui uplands can provide noticeable relief to the uninitiated. Evenings are accordingly cooler where the humidity is lower.

Remember that in humid conditions sweating becomes a far less effective mechanism for our bodies to cool themselves. The typical physiological response to internal heat generation is to sweat more. One result is that clothing can rapidly become sweat laden. Combat this by bringing lightweight shorts, shirts that breathe and wick well, and drink at least one water bottle an hour to sustain endurance. After your ride, be wary of dehydrating alcoholic beverages and load up on water and juices instead (or, as well). I found that a small amount of nearly weightless sugar-free Kool Aid makes sipping a 2-liter bottle of water each evening a more enjoyable experience.

The wind does blow in paradise. If fact, sometimes it howls. If you're going in the same direction as the wind this can mean cruising effortlessly at 30 mph. Yahoo! If you're riding into a stiff easterly, this means cranking along in low gear at 7 mph downhill. Yuck!

Generally the trade winds dominate the climate. These global wind patterns result from unequal solar heating of areas in lower latitudes directly beneath the sun which receive more energy than do regions at higher latitudes.

As the heated air rises, cooler air rushes in to fill the void. Accordingly, the northeasterly trades tend to be stronger and more persistent in the summer when this differential is greatest north of the equator. On Maui, Hawaii, and Moloka'i the trades are further intensified over the central isthmuses where the surface flow of air is constricted and funneled into a small pass between two mountain masses. The practical result is that riding from Ma'alaea or Kihei to Kahului on Maui and from Papohaku to Kaunakakai on Moloka'i can become a grinding challenge of will and perseverance that will truly test your zen of bicycle riding. On the Big Island of Hawaii the experience is enhanced with a 3,000-foot climb as well.

But fear not. There are things you can do to mitigate the effects of this nefarious succubus. The winds seldom blow full strength around the clock, often calming shortly after sunset and not gaining full strength until 3 or 4 hours after sunrise. Getting an early start can be a great help. Furthermore, strong trades are episodic and are prone to occasional several-days-long periods of calm. Remember, too, that though the winds may howl across the isthmuses, they are only 4 to 20 miles across and that elsewhere the Trades are weakened by buffering roadside forests.

Should you find yourself riding northwards with a strong tail wind one day, rejoice not. Instead get quickly to wherever you are going. Southerly winds, known as Kona Winds for the direction of their origin, generally from Kona on the Big Island to the south, are generated by strong Pacific storm systems and often herald a day or two of torrentially wet weather. The best thing to do in this case is to check out the local weather forecast, by recorded phone message or in the Honolulu Advertiser newspaper, and either run for a dry side of your island or hunker down in a town and wait out the storm.

It does rain in paradise, that's how it stays so green. There are two prevalent rain patterns. The first is driven by trade winds which pile up moist air on the eastern slopes of the islands and bring windward showers. The Hana coast of Maui, the Halawa area of Moloka'i, the Hilo side of Hawaii, and the whole eastern half of Kauai are most affected by this pattern. The cloudier the sky is generally, the more likely there will be windward showers. On Maui these showers reach around the Haleakala to the north as far as Baldwin Beach and upland Makawao to the north and around to Kipahulu to the south. Both the Hana Highway and the gravel portion of the Pi'ilani Highway suffer wash-outs and slides from showers. The recorded outdoor report at 877-5111 contains road condition advisories. The Big Island is less severely affected in terms of infrastructure; however, it is such a huge land mass that it creates a good deal of its own weather. The summit area on Kauai is the consistently wettest place on earth.

The second pattern called convective showers occurs when the trades relax. As still air over the steamy coasts heats and rises, clouds form above as the rising hot, wet air cools. Given sufficient heat and humidity these clouds result in *mauka*, (inland showers). These showers can occur on any inland area of any of the islands. Often the clouds and showers simply serve to cool off a hot, still day and they clear off as they cool the land.

The Haleakala wrings most of the moisture from the air passing over it as do the west Maui Mountains. As a result, downwind Kihei and Ka'anapali tend to be dry. Island Lana'i lies in the rain shadow of both Maui mountain masses and is nearly desert-like as a result, as is western Moloka'i. On the Big Island, towering Mauna Loa and Mauna Kea protect the Kailua side of the island from passing showers.

Due to its low latitude, days are never extremely long in Hawaii. At the winter solstice in late December the year's shortest day sees sunrise about 7 A.M. and sunset around 5 P.M. In late June the longest days begin near 5:30 A.M. and dark comes just after 7:30 P.M. If you're camping, a good book and a lantern (candle) can make long evenings considerably more enjoyable.

Your Bike: Love It? Leave It? Rent It?

Perhaps the most difficult and important decision you will have to make before you leave home is whether or not to take your bicycle to Hawaii with you. The two devils that will haunt you are first, the chance that those highly trained professional airline baggage handlers might accidentally drop your beloved from the wing tip squarely upon its deraileur, AAAHHHH! The second devil of course plays against the first, do you dare trust your vacation, not to mention your buns, to a bike you hardly even know?

Your decision must be your own, but whatever you decide here are some hints to help you through the process.

First, the airlines now uniformly charge a minimum of $50 to transport your bicycle, each way. To add insult to injury, they all make you sign an agreement absolving them from any damage that might befall your precious cargo.

There are steps you can take to minimize the chance of damage. Don't leave your packs or anything heavy on the bike. The increased weight makes a hard drop more likely to flatten a rim. Similarly, don't deflate your tires. Hard tires help protect your wheels. You may elect to remove your wheels; this is a good strategy to save your rims, but it leaves your back shifter horribly exposed. Building your own box from double-thickness furniture cardboard is another good measure, however, you still need to get your bike home after your trip, more than likely in one of the flimsy bike boxes the airlines will sell you for $10 plus tax. If you do build your own box, remember that its combined height, width, and thickness must be no more than 120 inches. Double-check this figure with your air carrier before beginning box construction.

There are commercially made, hard shell bike shipping cases available. Most require some disassembly, often including removing your hubs. Nashbar Cycling Supply Catalog offers such a case for $280; call 1-800-627-4227 for information. Check with your airline about long-term storage of the case while you are on vacation. If you are spending any time in a hotel near an airport, they might also store the case for you.

One other allowable strategy with some airlines is to package your bike in a sturdy bag. While on one hand this seems to leave your pride and joy horribly exposed: one the other hand, a bag makes it impossible for the airlines to stack other baggage on top of your bike and demands some special handling.

In any case you will need to do some disassembly. You will at least need to remove your pedals to make your bike more slender. You will likely have to drop your seat and handle bars to their minimum height. Mark the posts before you do this to aid reconfiguration upon arrival.

Rentals

There is an alternative to subjecting your cherished bike to these tortures. There are now a number of companies in Hawaii that rent bicycles, several of them quite reputable. The availability of rentals varies from island to island. There are no rentals available on Moloka'i and Lana'i; however, several businesses rent bikes on Maui, a short ferry ride away from these two smaller islands. Similarly, rentals are a little scarce on Kauai, but plentiful on both Hawaii and Oahu. Each Islands' introductory section discusses specific rental possibilities.

The down side of renting is that your body will be thrown onto a strangely configured machine, violating the intimate fit you've developed with your own bicycle after months of grueling conditioning. Stories of entire seasons being lost to young professional racers as a result of recklessly mounting a minutely reconfigured training bike come to mind. Of course, you may not have spent several hundred hours training in the month prior to your vacation so this may not be as important to you.

When making arrangements to rent, be certain that the shop knows that you want to use the bike for touring. A rear rack is essential, and smooth, hard tires roll much more easily than do soft knobby mud grippers. Inspect the bike carefully and fit it to you carefully. Ask about simple repair and adjustment operations if the bike is unfamiliar to you (all bikes have their idiosyncrasies). Also be clear about potential damage charges and determine mutually agreeable procedures in case of mechanical failure. Before you leave home find out if the shop rents pumps and tire patch kits. This is by far the most common type of break down and you should be self sufficient for tire repair. Bring your own pump and patch kit from home if necessary. Also make certain that the bike has water bottles, or at least two bottle cages and bring your own bottles from home if need be. Hawaii is hot and humid and you will need to replace liquid lost through sweat. Buy large bottles if you don't already have them.

Rental Checklist
1. Do they have a bike your size?
2. What is the weekly rental rate?
3. What make of bike is available in your size?
4. Does the rental have a back rack and a front rack if you want one?
5. Does the rental come with a repair kit?
6. Does the rental come with a tire pump, and, if you need to bring one from home, are the tube valves Schraeder or Presta size?

7. Does the shop deliver and pick up either you or the bike?
8. Does the shop offer road assistance or guarantee of quality of their cycles?
9. Does the shop charge for regular wear incurred while touring?
10. Does the bike have bottles and cages? If not, does the frame have braze-ons for two bottle cages. Don't accept a bike that will not accommodate at least two bottles.
11. If the bike has straight handlebars, does it also have bar ends? Bar ends aid your climbing ability and allow several different hand positions to help minimize "bikers palsy," numbness in the hands.

Repairs

A competent cycle tourist should be able to make minor repairs and adjustments to an ailing bike. The most likely mechanical breakdown is a flat tire and you should be comfortable patching and re-inflating a flaccid tube. Although on a recent 600-mile Hawaiian tour I didn't suffer a single flat tire, the islands are home to thousands of thorn-studded *kiawe* acacia trees and nearly as many bottle-chucking motorists.

Toward this end you may want to take a simple bicycle maintenance class. Knowledge of bike maintenance can give you an important feeling of self-confidence. Check with your local bike shop or Parks and Recreation Department for information on classes. You will also need a repair kit with at least these few tools:

1. A 6 inch or 8 inch adjustable wrench. Although these have many uses, they are especially good for removing and reinstalling your pedals for shipment.
2. Pliers.
3. A set of plastic or metal tire irons.
4. A patch kit stocked with adequate patches.
5. Any Allen wrenches that your bike might need.
6. A small amount of metal wire just in case.
7. Duct tape; good for improvising any number of emergency repairs.
8. A spare inner tube. Sometimes a patch just isn't possible.

Optional:
9. A spare tire.
10. A spoke wretch to true your wheels.
11. A chain tool and spare links to repair a broken chain.
12. A small screwdriver or Swiss Army knife.

Repair Shops

Sometimes a repair is just too much to fix yourself. Fortunately there are several good repair shops on Maui, Oahu, Kauai, and Hawaii; however, on Moloka'i and Lana'i you're pretty much on your own. Each Chapters' introduction contains a listing of bike shops.

If you should suffer a complete breakdown far away from any of these shops, remember that hitchhiking is illegal in Hawaii, and it's probably been a very long time since anyone has been arrested for such activity. Keep in mind too, that there are some shuttles running about the islands and there is almost always cab service available.

What To Bring

Entire books have been written on how to bike tour. If you are a novice and want to be assured of having a vacation rather than an adventure, do some additional reading on the subject. If, on the other hand, you're an experienced tourer-hiker-camper, this discussion should cover the necessary basics to ensure preparedness.

Cycle Computers: The route logs in this book contain sufficient references to landmarks that a bicycle computer/odometer is not necessary; however, using an odometer will help you both to navigate and to pace yourself as you ride. Cycle computers can be purchased at any bike store for as little as $25. Many now have tool-free installation designs and are no more complicated than setting a digital watch. All computers require you to tell it your tire size as this is variable from bike to bike. Direction booklets include diameter-circumference charts so that all you need know is the tire size, which is imprinted on the tire side-wall.

If you intend to rent a bike while on the islands for extensive use, you can bring a computer with you, or buy one at a local bicycle shop on the islands.

You may want to bring a light for your bike. There are tunnels across the Poli on Ochu and one in Maui where lights will increase your visibility. Lights also allow night riding, though highway night riding is generally unsafe anywhere but on Lauai and Molokai.

One of the most important items you need to bring is what I refer to as my apartment. I assemble my tent, sleep sack, and sleeping pad in a single bundle. I secure and compress these items together with two 1-inch wide nylon binding straps to make a compact if rather heavy bundle which rides well on the top of my rear rack. The perfect tent to take to Hawaii would be summer weight with good ventilation for those warm, humid nights. It should also be completely waterproof for the occasional tropical shower or even storm. Several companies make tents especially for cyclists with shorter poles designed to fit more easily upon bike racks. While these are nice, they aren't necessary. If you already own even a vaguely appropriate tent, save yourself the expense and go with it.

Your sleep sack needs to keep you warm down to 55° F. In a closed tent, this isn't very cold in the world of down and fiberfill sleeping bags. I save myself the bulk of hauling my down bag, instead I take a sleep sack made from a single flat sheet folded and sewn at the foot and halfway up one side. Unless you're going up the Haleakala and spending the night at chilly Hosmer Grove, this is all the bag you will probably need.

A good sleeping pad will be well worth the weight and expense. It will help keep you warmer on cool nights and provide you with a much better night's sleep. I also bring a small pillow with me. You can spend $35 on a small down pillow from an outdoor catalog, or go to most any large fabric or craft store and buy a 7" fiberfill pillow for about $5.

In order to carry all of the stuff you need, you must have packs to put it in. Bike packs, also called panniers, should be waterproof and highly visible to passing cars. Your local bike shop will gladly sell you a set starting at about $90, and you can easily spend up to $145 for a set. Fortunately for the neophyte cyclist, many people spend $100 on packs then realize that they really don't enjoy riding their bikes at all. Used sporting goods stores are, therefore, a great alternative and less expensive source for packs.

Some folks use only one set of packs on the back of their bike. Once you try to pack all of your stuff in these seemingly impossibly tiny bags you realize why those folks you saw riding the other day had additional packs on the front. I personally see the space limitation imposed upon me by these small-ish packs as good governors on the amount of stuff I take. The fact is, I can fit nearly all I need for an extended tour in my two small rear packs.

"Nearly all . . ."? Well, yeah. I also use, and recommend, handlebar bags. These are a perfect compromise between no front packs, and huge front packs. Handlebar bags fit on a metal rack that secures to your bars. Most hold about one-half of a cubic foot of gear which is enough for a camera, a rain jacket, your wallet, sun visor or screen, the day's munchies, and a copy of this book. All of these vital daily needs are stored accessibly at your fingertips in a handlebar bag. Bags sell for about $40 new.

If you've never ridden with full packs before, make sure you load up your bike before the trip and practice a bit. Your bike will not handle as responsively, especially at low speeds. Front packs and handlebar bags can cause some shimmy in the front of the bike and make handless riding if not impossible, at least fool-hardy.

Be cautious at first with high-speed turns. With a considerably greater load your tires may behave differently, "rolling" sideways during curves. Your bike will also be slower to start from a stop. However, once rolling, you may find that your bike holds speed and balances better, your inertial force is considerably greater when loaded. I feel almost protected, surrounded by my gear.

You also will need racks to hold your packs. Make sure you bring your bike to the shop when you buy your racks. Some bikes have braze-on nibs to fasten racks to your frame, others don't. To fit the dropped configuration of some mountain bikes, some racks are built with modifications in order to make the rack-bed fit horizontally. Your rack-bed should be perfectly horizontal when installed properly.

You should also consider adding fenders at this time if you don't already have them. Fenders do add weight; however, they also keep road gunk off your bike, your stuff, and you. I've never wished that mine were gone.

Now down to details.

Clothing

You should have at least two pair of good, lightweight padded bike shorts. Watch for sales and you can usually get them for as little as $20. Tops should have protective elbow length sleeves. Whether you deny the reality of Ozone munching CFCs in the upper atmosphere or not, all day is a long time for us *haoles* (see language section for translation) to have our shoulders exposed to the tropical sun. Second-degree sunburns can seriously mar a Hawaiian vacation. While $45 synthetic fabric bike jerseys may look very cool, I've yet to meet one whose wicking ability can keep up with my sweating ability in 90 degree heat with 90% humidity. Instead, I recommend bringing two or three cotton T-shirts, the thinner the better.

In case of rain, a Suplex jersey will shield you from the elements better than a cotton T, but a short sleeve polypropylene top will do even better. I've ridden comfortably all day in a cool Oregon coast rain wearing only a polypropylene shirt as a top. I find that Gore-Tex and other micropermiables are overwhelmed by perspiration and I end the day wet from the inside. If rain is a real concern, try pairing a polypro top with a bike poncho which allows great ventilation.

At the end of each day, when I hit the showers, I take my day's riding clothes with me and hand wash them. In the Hawaiian heat it's rare that they aren't dry for the next day if I need them. For the purpose of line drying expediency, I recommend lightweight synthetic blend cycling socks.

Before you climb into the shower at the end of your day, climb out of your riding shoes which, ideally, are touring style and cleatless. You should plan on being able to do some serious walking in your touring shoes. Then slip into your sport sandals. I recommend these because they are light, small, cool, and will stand up to considerable hiking.

Bike gloves are a matter of personal taste. They are normally sized to fit around the girth of your hand between your thumb and first knuckles. Finger length is, therefore, irrelevant. While handlebar tape padding improves constantly and mountain bike grips are also well cushioned, I don't see any reason to spend money on anything other than gel padded gloves. Gel pads, though more expensive, absorb shock and vibration without peer. The extra $10 in cost is easily made up by not suffering loss of sensation in my fingers for several days.

Some sort of sun visor is also highly recommended for cycling in Hawaii. Without it, your nose will be exposed to tens of hours of brutal tropical solar radiation. Unprotected, the result resembles a badly over-ripe pomegranate. There are several types of detachable helmet visors on the market these days starting at about $12. I bought a baseball style cap at the second-hand store, cut the top out of it and hemmed the ragged edge. It works great under my helmet and at the beach.

Helmet? Yes, I said helmet. If you think they look silly, trot on down to the head injury clinic to see how slick you could look without one. Snell and A.N.S.I. approved helmets are available at most bike shops and large discount stores. You needn't pay over $20 for perfectly good head protection.

Generally, the more you spend, the better the ventilation and the less the weight.

I also find sunglasses helpful when touring. They protect eyes from burning sun, stinging wind, and unidentified flying debris.

Remember to bring a few items of comfortable clothing for lounging around camp, or the resort lounge depending on your bent. Remember that Hawaii is a casual place and that clean casual clothing will get you into just about any place you care to go if accompanied by the appropriate credit card. Some pocketed and/or pleated nylon shorts are crunchably packable, light, and look nice over your bikers' legs. Running shorts with liners are nearly perfect for Hawaiian lounging and both types of shorts can double as swimsuits.

Jog-bras are also highly versatile items for riding, swimming, and sunning. Think twice about relying on them as your only top. The sun is strong here.

Camping Gear

Beyond your sleeping gear already discussed, you will also need a kitchen. Foremost, you need a stove. Remember that airlines do not allow you to carry or check fuel cartridges onto the plane. The second consideration for selecting your stove beyond small size is availability of compatible fuel bottles. See the introductions to the individual islands for the location of outdoor supply stores.

You will also need some kind of cooking vessels and eating utensils. Your local outdoor supply store should stock a wide variety. Keep it small and light.

While at your outdoor store pick up some form of water sterilization preparation. The parks at Halawa and Pala'au both recommend treating water. Several of the parks on the Big Island also have water that is best treated. Iodine pills are small and effective against all sorts of literally gut-wrenching bacterium.

Nights are every bit as dark in Hawaii as they are in Montana. A small candle lantern to read by and a flashlight to avoid becoming one of those things that go bump in the night will both add much to your camping experience. As always, keep it small and light.

The unofficial State Bird of Hawaii is the mosquito. These tireless vampires seem especially fond of the blood of the *haoles* whose race originally introduced these pests to paradise. To avoid being carried away to their lair in the waning twilight, bring repellent. Because shower facilities aren't always available, buy a repellent that you can live with for an extended period. Many people have had success with citronella-based repellents.

The occasional unavailabilty of showers also suggests the value of a small bottle of no-rinse liquid soap. After a day of grunting in the saddle under a hot sun, a dry bath can be a blessing for both you and your travel companions.

Equipment Checklist
- 2 pair riding shorts. Keep one pair with you on the plane to change into before landing.
- 2 or 3 riding shirts.
- 1 nice shirt.
- 1 presentable pair of shorts.
- 1 pair running shorts.
- 3 pair lightweight socks.
- 1 pair sport sandals.

- 1 pair riding shoes.
- 1 helmet.
- 1 pair riding gloves.
- Sunglasses.
- Sun visor.
- Light windproof or waterproof jacket.
- 1 polypropylene shirt, long underwear style.
- 1 tent with rain-proof capability.
- 1 sleep sack of the necessary weight.
- 1 sleeping pad.
- 1 pillow, travel size.
- 1 camp stove.
- Matches in waterproof container.
- Cooking vessels.
- Eating utensils.
- Flashlight.
- Candle lantern.
- A good book.
- Insect repellent.
- No-rinse soap.
- Water purification tablets.
- Small containers of salt, pepper, and your favorite spices.
- Short roll of toilet paper (smash it flat).
- Rag to clean bike (I bring an aging pair of socks and use them to clean my bike after I've worn them, then discard).
- Multi-implemented pocket knife.
- Bike tools: Allen wrenches, adjustable wrench to remove and install pedals, innertube patch kit, tire irons, a spare tube, 1 or 2 feet of duct tape, pliers.
- Toothbrush.
- Toothpaste.
- Shampoo. Conditioner helps tame road-ravaged hair.
- Smallish bath towel. Thin towels dry faster.
- Smallish beach towel (optional). Can be rolled up with sleeping pad.
- Personal hygiene items.
- This book.

If you forget something, don't worry, Hawaii is a civilized land with plenty of stores to supply you.

Politics

Maui County lies in the geographic center of the State of Hawaii. Maui County is comprised of three different islands, all with different interests. Within the island units there is further factionalization. Thrown together, the people make a potent stew.

Geographically, it makes some sense to include all three islands as one political unit. Maui, Lana'i, and Moloka'i are so close physically that the narrow straits between them nearly forms a small sea. In fact, during ice ages when glaciers lock up ocean water and the sea level drop as much as 300 feet, the three islands are actually joined into one large island with extensive low lands in the middle. This proximity is unique among Hawaiian islands.

One pleasant result is the frequent ferry service from Maui to Moloka'i and Lana'i. These ferries are also unique amongst the other islands of this ocean state.

Each island, however, has a very different character and history. Maui had always been the home of powerful Kings, always in contention with the Ali'i of Oahu for dominance over Moloka'i and to some degree the less valuable Lana'i. When the *haoles* came in force in the second decade of the nineteenth century, Lahaina became the principal port for whalers and other ships. Maui quickly felt the ravages of drunken, syphilitic seamen on one hand, and cultural destruction at the hands of Christian sects competing to introduce the natives to the foreign concepts of "guilt" and "hell" on the other hand. The rich remains of nineteenth-century Christendom, in the form of quaint white frame churches, are often built on foundations made from the stones of destroyed Hawaiian *heiaus*, or shrines.

Water-poor Lana'i remained little more than a fishing colony for both the Hawaiians and the *haole*. Cattle grazing was introduced in the later half of the 1800s with disastrous effects on island flora, fauna, and soil which suffered erosion.

This century saw the destruction of the eastern aquifer by a short-lived sugar plantation operation, and in the 1970s the slow demise of the once-dominant pineapple plantation. Currently, Lana'i consists of 2,200 souls, many of whom are of Philippian stock, workers imported to work in the fields. Industry is limited to cattle grazing and tending the well-to-do at the island's two hyper-expensive resorts.

Moloka'i has been led down a different path. The island suffered early the ravages of sandalwood logging which hastened deforestation and lead the ali'i to act dishonorably toward the people who had supported them for so long. The result was a breakdown in the traditional kapu system of civil behavior and mass starvation and drunkenness among the common people who uncomprehendingly signed away the rights to their kuleanas, long held family lands.

Not long after the sandalwood ran out, *haoles* began grabbing all possible lands and grazing cows and goats. The resultant denudation of slopes caused severe soil erosion which was, in turn, deposited along the shallow south coast. The sediment silted-in and destroyed the fishponds so vital to the native economy. Western Moloka'i was made a desert wasteland, useless until *haole* concerns began importing water from the eastern mountains via a series of tunnels, canals, and pipes. Currently these water works take much of the available water from central homelands to feed the west end Kalua Koi golf course.

In 1892, Queen Liliuokalani ascended to the Hawaiian throne just as the McKinley Tariff was instituted. The tariff on non-American sugar was designed to punish the Spanish for allegedly brutal acts against the people of their Cuban colony. In Hawaii, it resulted in a depression. The *haole* land holders used the cause as a rallying point and on January 13, 1893, they effected a coup d'etat. Liliuokalani ceded the government under protest, believing that American courts would grant her relief. They didn't. Royal lands were converted to State lands, and in 1898 both houses of the United States Congress approved annexation by simple majorities.

Through a series of illegal land grabs around the turn of the century, the American Sugar Company, predecessor to the Moloka'i Ranch, accumulated nearly all of the lands of the western half of the island. Cane operations had exhausted the aquifer so the Cook Company, along with Dole, Delmonte, and Libby Foods, began growing dessication-resistant pineapple. This enterprise eventually failed due to foreign competition. However, vestiges of this plantation culture still remain in Ho'olehua and Maunaloa town which is being rapidly raised by the Moloka'i Ranch.

Eastern Moloka'i is divided into lands held by the Moloka'i Ranch, a marvelous State forest preserve, and homestead lands set aside for natives in 1921. With the exception of the Pu'u o Hoku Ranch at the far eastern tip of the island, the further east you go, the more Hawaiian the lands become. This area has nurtured the nascent Sovereign Hawaii movement. The movement is evident in the militancy among those who live here; camouflage trucks with gun racks, illegal "Sovereign Nation" license plates, bumper stickers, and No Trespassing signs all attest to the determination of the Native people to re-assert their claim to these islands. In the summer of 1995, tribal police served several state officials with papers ordering them to appear before Hawaiian Native court on charges of treason.

All of these disparate interests come together at the county government offices in Wailuku, Maui. It is a potent mix.

Generally, citizens on Lana'i and Moloka'i feel that they are under-represented due to their relatively small populations. Maui, meanwhile, must attempt to build an infrastructure to accommodate the 2.2 million tourists it receives each year while the State is struggling with an ever-growing budget deficit.

With the generous proportions of Pearl Harbor as its chief asset, Oahu became the site of the *haole* capital, Honolulu. This primate city has grown into a bewildering behemoth and is now plagued by many of the problems faced by other major U.S. urban centers. There is homelessness and random acts of violence, and gang activity continues to grow. Waikiki, the tourist center within Honolulu, has maintained a feeling of relative safety; though watching the working girls work the Japanese tourists on the strip has become one of the most entertaining things to do at night.

Kauai sits isolated from the other main islands to the northwest, out of sight of its nearest neighbor Oahu. Kauai was the last of the islands to submit to Kamehameha's dynasty. It was also the first landfall made by Captain James Cook in 1788. Today Kauai still has a large sugar cane industry due to a plentiful water supply. Kauai also has granted homelands to natives near the commercial center of Lihue. Though the tourism industry is still rebuilding from the ravages of Hurricane Iniki, there is a palpably restive feeling amongst the young Native population and the island seems ripe for a wave of Sovereign Nation activism.

Hawaii, at the far southeastern end of the State, was home to Kamehameha. Its huge landscape proved a good training ground for the unification campaign Kamehameha was to wage; however, its location doomed it to political obscurity. Though there are well-sited Homelands above Kailua-Kona and near Hilo, an overwhelming majority of non-park land is locked up in the Parker Ranch, reputedly the largest privately held ranch in the United States. In the face of such blatant capital concentration, the Natives' spirituality is bolstered by the vigor of the Goddess Pele, nowhere as evident as here, in the ever active volcano.

As you ride around these gentle islands, it is good to be aware that you are on land that was taken from a thriving nation. In the process the Hawaiian culture was nearly destroyed. Now the Nation is beginning to find itself again, and heroically is reasserting its validity. Fortunately, as you pedal the placid shores and mountains of these multifaceted islands, most of these controversies will elude you, unless you look for them.

Language

Pronunciation: Hawaiian is a highly phonetic language, it sounds very much as it looks. The one very common exception is the letter "w" which is pronounced as English speakers pronounce the letter "v" so that "Hawaii" is pronounced "Havaii." Another tricky point in pronunciation is the glottal stop signified by an apostrophe, often in the middle of a word. It is spoken as a brief pause like that in the exclamation "oh-oh". So Kapa'a town is pronounced "Kapa-a."

Hawaiian is a language of compound words. Short fundamental words are joined to make longer words of complex meaning. The results are long words full of vowels that may look intimidating to the uninitiated. Break the word down into syllables and speak each one at a time, then work them together. Once you hear the lyricism of a word, you'll likely remember how to say it next time.

Below is a glossary of some commonly heard and seen Hawaiian words:

Ali'i: The ruling class in traditional society.
Aloha: A salutation for both greeting and leaving.
Brah or braddah: Brother or close male friend.
Da kine: Modern slang for either "the kind" or "the good kind."
Hale: Home or structure.
Haole: Caucasian person, or off-islander.
Hapa: Half.
Heiau: A temple site, often marked by a flat raised platform of piled stone.
Kahuna: A person possessing a powerful spirit, formerly of the professional class.
Kane: Man, men, male mate.
Kapu: Once a system of forbidden actions, or laws. Now more often used to
    signify "keep out." Obey it.
Kokua: Help.
Kuleana: Traditional family farm land.
Lanai: A covered porch.

Mahalo: Thank you. Use this word often.
Mana: Good spiritual energy given by the gods.
Makai: Oceanward or towards the edge.
Mauka: Inland or towards the center.
Mauna: Mountain.
Mea: Red.
Moana: Ocean.
Ohana: Family, in Hawaii this refers to the extended version.
Ono: Yum, the best.
Pakalolo: Marijuana, also known as Maui wowy.
Pali: Cliff.
Paniolo: Cowboy, of which there are many in the ranch lands.
Wai: Fresh water.
Wiki: Quickly. I've found that "wiki" is a relative term, and that fast usually
    doesn't mean the same thing in the tropics as it does in the mid-latitudes.

About the Maps
   The maps in this book are meant to be used as a rudimentary guide.
There are additional maps available which provide considerably more detail.
The United States Geological Survey (USGS) publishes topographic maps
with varying contour intervals. Their 1:24,000 scale maps, known as
"quads" are large scale, about 2 inches to the map mile. While extremely detailed, with the exception of Moloka'i and Lana'i, you must purchase several maps to cover any single tour. USGS maps may be purchased at many
bookstores or ordered from the USGS. Contact them at: USGS Information Services, P.O. Box 25286, Denver, CO 80225.
   There are also some fine privately produced maps widely available at
book stores.
   There are also many additional comprehensive guide books available. Nearly all of these contain maps of specific areas of interest. I
would encourage you to peruse the travel section in your favorite book
store to see if there isn't an additional guidebook to supplement this
one. Most books specialize their content to appeal to certain markets.
The bibliography in this book briefly reviews several of the current
publications. If you are planning to camp and cook for yourself, this
book may be all you need.
   The aerial-view maps included in this book are of varying scale and ori-
entation. Each has a graphic scale bar and north arrow to help you orient
yourself. The profile maps also have varying scales, both vertical and horizontal. However, the scale on each profile is clearly labeled. Pay careful attention to the scales. A vertical inch on one map may represent 500 feet,
while on another map, one inch may equal 6,000.
   Never interpret the steepness of the profile to be equal to the steepness
of the road. In all cases, the vertical scale is exaggerated so as to communicate
gradients in meaningful ways. Again, due to vastly different vertical scales, a
200-foot climb may seem huge if it is the only hill on a flat route segment,

while the profile of the 10,000-foot climb up the Haleakala looks very gentle in relation to the route as a whole.

If you are not accustomed to using topographic information, determine the height of some of the hills in your riding region and ride them. In doing so, not only will you get in shape for your tour, you will become familiar with what a 500-foot hill feels like. This way you will be able to judge tour difficulty for yourself. Keep in mind also that modern highway engineering accepts a 6 percent grade as the maximum acceptable slope, and that most of the highways in Hawaii numbered with two digits meet that standard.

As the aerial maps contain only a portion of all potential information about the landscape, so too do the profiles. Generally, the profiles do not depict route elevation changes less than five to ten percent of the segment's total elevation variation. Inclusion of all such information can make maps confusing. Rest assured, if there is a significant climb or descent relative to the whole segment, it will be depicted.

The following symbols are commonly used in the accompanying maps.

Direction of Travel

The route guides in this book are written to be traveled in the direction indicated in the route title. Riders traveling in the opposite direction can easily follow the guides with some careful reading. A *left* turn in one direction must be read as a *right* turn if travel is reversed. The route log often addresses what comes after a given point, so counter-directional riders must read ahead and reverse the log. For example, the log may indicate the beginning of a two-mile descent beginning at mile 14.7. Riders proceeding backwards through the log must read ahead and interpret this to mean that at mile 16.7 they will begin an ascent 2 miles long ending at mile 14.7.

The Manele Bay Resort's privately owned campground is just 100 feet away from the beach of Honopo'e Bay. Dolphins share this sun drenched beach with the local surfers. A $5 per night camping fee is charged, whereas a $300 per night fee is charged at the resort beyond.

23

Chapter 2

Maui

Maui is the second most visited Hawaiian island behind busy Oahu with its famous Waikiki district. Maui is also the second-largest island behind the massive island Hawaii to the south. And Maui is the second youngest of the islands with the most recent flow occurring in the mid 1700s above La Perouse Bay. However, Mauiians will not accept any ranking below first and demonstrate their pride in their island with the slogan "Maui no ka oi," Maui is the best. In fact Maui offers the traveler an astoundingly wide range of attractions from the posh resorts of the Ka'anapali coast to the somnambulant charm of forest-draped Hana, with the volcanic moon-scapes and green pasturelands of the Haleakala volcano in between.

For the cyclist, Maui offers more bike friendly miles and more varied riding opportunities than any other island. There are two grand loops, one around the west Maui mountains and the other around the Haleakala. There is a paved ascent up the literally breathtaking 10,000-foot Haleakala. There are flat rides across the central isthmus and along the coasts with numerous accessible beaches, and there are challenging ascents to the less-touristed uplands.

Maui is currently in the throes of a tourism industrial revolution. In the mid-eighties the state recognized that the tourist trade was stretching geographic and logistic limitations on Oahu and designated Maui to be the next Hawaiian tourist mecca. At the time they set the goal of 20 million tourist visits to Maui by 1995. Though the trade has fallen short of the goal, it is not far short, and the smallish Kahului Airport is as busy as many urban airports on the Mainland.

Getting There

A benefit of this development plan is that there are now numerous direct flights to Maui from several western cities. Not only does this save you money by skipping the inter-island shuttle, it also saves you precious vacation time. While the flight from Honolulu to Kahului takes only about 1/2 hour, making connections in Honolulu is seldom done in less than 2 hours. If your flight to Honolulu isn't contiguous with your flight to Maui, you may also encounter an additional surcharge of $50 for your bicycle on the island hop.

The flight from the west coast of the Mainland takes about 5 hours, and can cost anywhere from $400 to $700 depending upon season and fare wars.

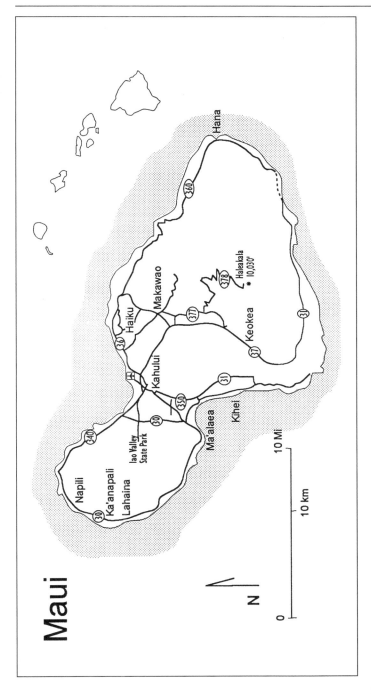

Maui

N

0   10 Mi

10 km

Hana

360

Makawao

Haiku

30

377

378

Haleakala
10,030'
*

Keokea

37

31

Kahului

350

31

30

Iao Valley
State Park

340

Napili

Ka'anapali

Lahaina

Ma'alaea

Kihei

30

Low season is anytime the weather is as good where you are as it is in Hawaii, and the kids are in school. Otherwise, it is pretty reliably "high season" for the airlines. Seem unfair? Try getting there without an airline.

The Kahului Airport is manageably small, and like all other airports in the islands is delightfully open air, delightful that is, if you aren't wearing a wool suit. To avoid uncomely excessive perspiration, keep your warm weather riding togs on the top of your carry-on bag and change before the plane lands. There are large open areas near the baggage claim where you can comfortably reassemble and adjust your bike. To avoid a sharp reprimand from airport security, don't ride your bicycle in the terminal.

Names and Numbers
• Hawaii Visitors Bureau: P.O. Box 1738, Kahului, HI, 96732, (871-8691), or 1-800-525-MAUI (6284) for a tourist packet.
• Area code 808 for all of Hawaii.
• Private bus line to Lahaina-Ka'anapali; 877-7308.
• Weather line, 24 hour recorded information for all of Maui/ 877-5111.
• As in all of Hawaii, dial 911 for emergency response.

Camping
There is a plethora of camping options available on Maui. In addition to wild camping and one private campground, there are camps administered by Maui County, The State of Hawaii, and the National Park Department.

Maui County:
Write to Department of Parks and Recreation, Maui County, War Memorial Gym, 1580 Kaahumanu Avenue, Wailuku, Hawaii, 96793 or call at (808) 243-7389. The Gym is a few miles from the airport on the road from Kahului to Wailuku on the right just past the huge white canvas roofed Kaahumanu Mall. They're open Mon.-Fri. 8am-4pm.

Maui County currently offers two campsites. One at Baldwin Beach Park one mile west of Paia and about six miles east of the airport. The camping area is 50 feet from a busy highway and the showers are a five minute walk away. The second site is at Rainbow park, about 5 miles up Baldwin Avenue from Paia. Rainbow Park is fairly primitive and has only a chemical toilet and no fresh water source, save its namesake, the rainbows which frequent this quiet upland area. Water is available at the church 0.2 miles down the hill. See the Kahului-Haleakala Route description far more details. Reservations and permits are required at each, cost $3 per night, and can be purchased in advance by mail.

Maui County is currently planning to develop camping at Kanaha Beach Park, an agreeable beach site frequented by hordes of windsurfers. Kanaha is within walking distance of the airport, convenient, but noisy.

All County Parks close to camping for five days near the end of the month. The intent is to clear out squatters. The County can give you these dates for any particular month.

State of Hawaii:

Division of State Parks, P.O. Box 1049, Wailuku, Hawaii, 96793 or phone at (808) 244-5354. The office is located up Kaahumanu Avenue in Wailuku 2 miles beyond the War Memorial Gym at 54 High Street, downstairs.

Hawaii operates an incredibly scenic park and campground at Wainapanapa three miles north of Hana at the far end of the mind-boggling Hana Highway, approximately 50 miles from the airport. There are outrageous walks along the black lava coast to ancient burial grounds and *heiaus* (shrines), swimming at a small cove, good restrooms and open air, ambient temperature showers.

Polipoli Park high above upland Kula awaits the intrepid off-road biker at the end of a long series of switch-backs worthy of the gods.

State Parks are free. However, reservations are required. So write in advance to get your paperwork in order.

National Parks:

Camping at the two National Park sites is not only free, it doesn't even require a reservation. It is, however, first come, first served. There is a three day maximum stay at each site. Write: Haleakala National Park, P.O. Box 369, Makawao, Hawaii 96768 or phone (808) 572-7749 for tour and weather information.

Hosmer Grove Campground is just off the Haleakala Highway at 6,800 feet in elevation. It offers camping in a lovely grassy field surrounded by stands of exotic trees imported by Mr. Hosmer in an attempt to find a commercially viable crop tree. There are stand pipes with clean, cold water, but no showers.

The Oheo Gulch portion of the Haleakala National Park is located 12 miles beyond Hana on the islands' southern tip. Home of the "Seven Sacred Pools," a *haole* title coined to aid in the marketing of the area, Oheo Gulch offers great fresh-water swimming and wondrous hikes through mysterious bamboo forests to a high waterfall. There is no drinking water at the Park so you must bring it with you from Hana or purchase it from the nearby Park Headquarters for $.75 per liter. The campground itself is a huge mowed field with nice pit toilets and picnic tables. There are also several campsites below great old *ti* trees near the water's edge.

Private Camps:

There are two private camps on Maui, and they are as different as night and day.

Camp Pecosa, 18 miles from the Kahului airport and just six miles south of swinging Lahaina, is on west Maui's west side. Pecosa is especially popular with European campers and offers an interesting international mix. It also offers hot showers and a quiet, convenient place to camp.

There is also Windmills Park just east of Honolua Bay's prime snorkeling. The camp is owned by Maui Land and Pineapple Company and has no facilities. Call the Company at (808) 6696201 to arrange to pay your $5 per night fee.

Other Accommodations

YMCA Camp Keanae on the Hana coast overlooks the picturesque Keanae peninsula were several Hawaiian families are seeking to pursue their ancestors' way of life. Camp Keanae is an organizational camp and is often filled by large groups who make reservations far in advance. Though the facilities are rustic, the few hostel-style beds are under a roof in this often rainy region, and the location half way down the Hana Highway makes this an appealing stopover. Call well in advance if possible, (808) 242-9007.

There is also the Banana Bungalow Hostel at 310 North Market Street in Wailuku, (800) 846-7835 or 244-5090. Here you can get a bunk for less than $20, or a room for about $35. They offer organized trips which might allow you access to a lot of things you might not otherwise get to do if relying strictly on your bicycle for transportation.

There are, of course, numerous Bed and Breakfasts. Contact the Hawaii Visitors Bureau, 2270 Kalakaua Avenue, Honolulu, Hawaii 96815, (808) 923-1811 for references to B&B clearing houses. Or try All Island B&B, (800) 542-0344.

Camping Supplies

There is a huge K-Mart one mile down Keolani Place near the airport. There is also GasPro with all sorts of popular styles of cartridges for sale. To get there, continue straight for two blocks after Keolani Place turns into Dairy Road in front of the K-Mart. Turn right off Dairy Road onto Alamaha Street. After two blocks, turn right again. GasPro is at the end of the block on the right.

In Wailuku on Maui try Maui Sporting Goods at 92 Market Street near the Hostel and right on the way to Iao Valley State Park, phone them at 244-0011.

Groceries

With the exception of the remote east side of west Maui and the even more desolate south side of the Haleakala beyond Hana, groceries are readily available. There are huge supermarkets in Kahului-Wailuku, Kihei, and Lahaina. However, nearly every town has a grocery store. Directions to some supermarkets are contained in the various route descriptions, as are warnings of the absence of groceries.

Restaurants

A lot of people live on Maui, and even more visit the island, so as you might expect, there is no shortage of places to eat out. Lahaina is especially flush with restaurants of varying price and cuisine. Lahaina also features an arts street fair on Friday evenings complete with outdoor food booths. Kahului and Kihei both offer a wide range of restaurants with a special emphasis on American "cuisine" i.e. fast food franchises abound. Some of the resorts at Ka'anapali feature three-star restaurants in opulently beautiful settings.

Other Services
•Area Code: 808
•Bus: Trans Hawaiian leaves from the Kahului airport for Lahaina and Ka'anapali every hour, $13; call them at 877-7308.
•Emergency: 911 works throughout the islands.
•Ferries: The Maui Princess leaves from Lahaina for Moloka'i each day at 7 A.M. and 5 P.M. and begins the return trip from Kaunakakai, Moloka'i at 5:30 A.M. and 3:55 P.M.. Call them at (808) 661-8397 for reservations. Bikes are free and the fare is $35 each way. Expeditions at (808) 661-3756 begins the 45-minute trip from Lahaina to Manele Harbor on Lana'i each day at 6:45 A.M., 9;15 A.M., 12:45 P.M., 3:15 P.M., and 5:45 P.M.. The ferry begins the return trip at 8:00 A.M., 10:30 A.M., 2:00 P.M., 4:30 P.M., and 6:45 P.M.. The fare is $35 for you and $10 for your bicycle each way. Reserve a seat in high season.
•Weather: 877-5111 (surf conditions included).
•Visitor Information: 1727 Wili Pa Loop, Kahului, HA, (808) 244-3530, or at the Kahului airport, 877-3894.

Bicycle Rental
Kukui Activities Center: based in Kihei, the friendly folk at Kukui will deliver and pick up your rented mountain bike at the Kahului airport if you rent for at least one week. They charge $17 per day, $70 per week, and $170 for a month and feature current year Taleras GT bikes. Write to Kukui Activity Center, 1819 South Kihei Road, Building E, Kihei, Hawaii 96753, or call at (808) 875-1151.

South Maui Bicycles, also in Kihei offers road ready mountain bikes for $79 per week and touring road bikes for $110 per week. Some have rear racks, some don't. The owner cautioned me that touring is hard on their bikes, and that they charge for any damage the bike suffers, so review the bike carefully before leaving the shop. Contact them at 1913-C South Kihei Road, Kihei, HI 99753; (808) 874-0068.

Speedi Shuttle has two locations, one in Lahaina featuring Trek 830s and the other at Kahana north of Ka'anapali, which features Marin Hawk Hill bicycles. They have nearly 50 bikes to choose from, about half with racks. They also offer a few high-end road bikes. Contact them at P.O.Box 11000, Lahaina, HI 96761; (808) 875-8070.

West Maui Cycles, also in Kahana, offers free pick-up and delivery; a valuable service where public transportation is so limited and vacation time so precious. Contact them at 3600 Lower Honoapiilani Road, Suite H1, Kahana, HI (808) 669-1169.

There are two other rental agencies in Lahaina. Fun Bike Rentals at 193 Lahainaluna Road, Lahaina, HI (808) 661-3053 had a beautiful Masi racing bike in the rental rack out front. You could also try Maine-iac Cycles at 741 Wainee, Lahaina, HI (808) 661-8719.

In Kahului near the airport, try The Island Biker in the Kahului Shopping Center, phone (808) 877-7744. They rent 21-speed mountain bikes for $65 per week and offer a student discount.

Repair Shops

Sometimes a repair is just too much to fix yourself. Fortunately there are several good repair shops on Maui; however, on Moloka'i and Lana'i you're pretty much on your own.

In Kahului you have at least two options:

Island Biker: Located on the corner of Dairy Road, which is the road to the airport, and the Hana Highway 36. Though a small shop, they are often available to fix your bike on the spot. Phone them at 877-7744.

The Bike Shop: A few blocks west of Island Biker on the Hana Highway, this is a much larger store also within limping distance of the airport. 111 Hana Highway, Kahului, phone 877-5848.

In Kihei there are two more shops:

Island Biker: Yet another outlet. Call them at 875-7744.

South Maui Cycles: Rentals and repairs. They're at 1913-C, South Kihei Road, across from the big concrete whale. Call them at 874-0068.

In Paia on the road to Hana there's The Paia Bike Shop. A modest operation, this shop concentrates on repairs rather than sales. Like everything else in Paia, the repair may be a little laid back. Find them 2 blocks up Baldwin Avenue from the Hana Highway next to the Laundromat at 105 Baldwin Avenue, phone 579-8976.

In Lahaina go to Maine-iac Cycles at 741 Wainee Road, phone 661-8719. Or try Fun Bike Rentals at 193 Lahainaluna Road next to a great natural food store just two blocks off the center of Front Street.

Kahului Airport—Lahaina: The Short Route

The miles seem to fly by on this flat, often tradewind propelled ride. The Highways followed are busy, but the shoulders are especially generous, the traffic courteous, and seldom travels faster than 45 mph.

This route just brushes the southern edge of the residential city of Kahului before heading over the low hump of the central Maui isthmus. Along the way you can get a good look at pineapple and sugar cane still in the ground.

Six miles from the Airport the road merges with Highway 30 to Lahaina and you drop nearly to sea level as you pass Ma'alaea town whose chief industry is snorkeling excursions, mostly to tiny Molokini island just off the coast in southern Ma'alaea Bay.

Just beyond Ma'alaea roll over a series of small and very scenic hills hugging the jagged coast, finally passing through the only automobile tunnel in Maui County before dropping back down to the beach.

The final 10 miles into Lahaina is flat and features constant views of the rugged west Maui mountains, green sugar cane fields, and the islands Lana'i and Moloka'i across the channels. Yahoo!

Miles from Kahului	*Miles from Lahaina*
0.0	*23.3*

Begin on Keolani Place in front of the baggage claim area near the rental car desks. There is plenty of room there to reassemble your bicycle. Begin on Keolani Place (the airport road). The shoulder here is narrow, but the sidewalk is wide, little traveled, and has curb cuts.

1.2
22.1
Stay on Keolani past the intersection with Haleakala Highway 396.

1.4
21.9
Keolani Place becomes Dairy Road as it intersects Hana Highway 36. To your right before crossing Highway 36 is the Island Biker bike shop. They offer both bike rentals and quick repair in case the airlines have damaged your pride and joy. Three blocks to the right at 111 Hana Highway is The Bike Shop in case Island biker can't help.

1.6
21.7
Alamaha Street branches to the right. Alamaha provides access to a camping gas supply store (Gas Pro, 2 blocks down and 1 block right) and a really big Safeway Supermarket and numerous fast food outlets 0.9 miles directly ahead on Alamaha.

1.7
21.6
Watch for Maui Bagel and Deli nestled in a strip mall on your right. Try the Pineapple Bagels for breakfast. Yum.

2.1
21.2
Intersection with Highway 350 to Kihei and Makena. Dairy Road now becomes Kuihelani Highway, 380. Ride along the extremely generous shoulder for 4.6 miles as the road gently rises through fields of sugar cane covering the central Maui isthmus.

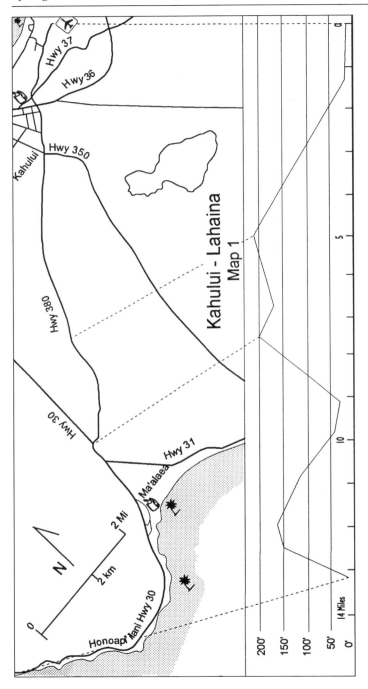

Kahului - Lahaina
Map 1

Hwy 37
Hwy 36
Hwy 350
Kahului
Hwy 380
Hwy 30
Hwy 31
Ma'alaea
2 Mi
2 km
N
0
Honoapi'ilani Hwy 30

200'
150'
100'
50'
0'

0
5
10
14 Miles

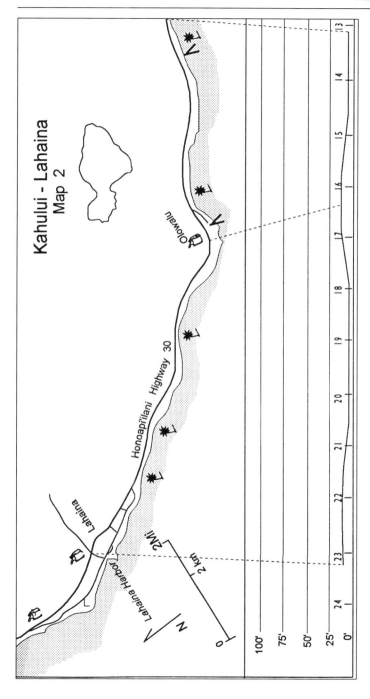

Kahului - Lahaina
Map 2

Honoapi'ilani Highway 30

Olowalu

Lahaina

Lahaina Harbor

N

0

2 Mi

2 Km

100'
75'
50'
25'
0'

13 14 15 16 17 18 19 20 21 22 23 24

33

3.2
20.1
The smallest of the major Hawaiian islands, Kahoolawe comes into view across a moderate strait. Until just a few years ago Kahoolawe had been infested with imported goats which denuded this dry island while dodging Naval bombers who used the island for gunnery practice. The island has since been returned to Native Hawaiian control, but it has taken years to clear the land of un-detonated armaments.

7.2
15.1
Intersection with Highway 30 and end of Highway 380. Turn left here and let the trade winds carry you down the hill to Ma'alaea. Notice how the hills above you become less verdant. As you travel south and west you enter the rain shadow of the west Maui mountains and the thorny, picturesque forest of imported acacia mesquite trees come to dominate the landscape.

9.0
14.3
Pass the second and most direct of three exits to Ma'alaea. Ma'alaea harbor is primarily a tourist facility featuring numerous snorkeling and sailing expeditions, many to tiny Molokini Island, a small crescent volcanic cone visible across Ma'alaea Bay. Ma'alaea also features three restaurants and a small market located in the seaward side of the condominium building closest to the harbor.

Over the next 4 miles the road hugs the sea cliffs as it dips and climbs through relative desert. Shoulders narrow a bit but are still generous. Traffic speed, as is the case all around Maui County, seldom exceeds 45 mph.

10.9
12.4
A well-signed view point on the right provides an excellent opportunity to dismount and watch for whales. I once was sitting on the beach near here reading a novel when I heard a most unearthly rumbled sigh. I looked up to see three adult humpback whales attempting to mate and breathing noisily not 100 feet away. The season begins in December and ends in May and Ma'alaea Bay is a favorite haunt.

12.5
10.8
Begin a short, level tunnel. There is a thoughtful sign warning motorists to watch for bikes. Don't rely on it. Stop. Turn on your lights. Wait for a break in traffic, which are thankfully frequent and sufficiently long. Then pedal fast.

12.6
10.7
End of the tunnel. If you're reading this, you've made it. Now turn off

your lights and coast down 0.6 miles as the highway begins a marvelous beach-side run into Lahaina.

13.2
10.1
Papalaua State Wayside. For the next 0.5 miles numerous camping spots line the Acacia-strewn beach. Although informal camping is officially illegal here, there are always plenty of tents and fisherpeople. Facilities are limited to a few picnic tables and some chemical toilets. No water is available.

16.2
7.1
Punahoa Beach extends for the next 0.6 miles and features some of the best shallow reef snorkeling on Maui. Unfortunately there are no showers here. I find dried salt water and vigorous cycling to be a most uncomfortable combination. In order to avoid chafing, try it only in limited quantities.

16.3
7.0
Camp Pecu sa. The entrance to this full-service private campground is marked by a small sign at the base of a Tsunami warning siren pole on the left side of the road shortly after the coast line curves away from the road. This is the only official camp spot within 20 miles in either direction and is conveniently close to Lahaina (6 miles distant).

16.7
6.6
Olowalu Market. A supermarket it's not. But they have the essentials covered. The market opens and closes early 6 A.M. to 7 P.M. most days, and the soda machines out front are always on.

For the next five miles the road stays near sea level as the beach appears and recedes behind cane fields.

17.0
6.3
Straight ahead in the distance the green and rugged mountains of east Moloka'i rise above the nearby cane.

19.8
3.5
Lanuipoko Wayside. Outdoor showers are available here as is good drinking water and less good rest rooms. This is a wonderful place to watch the sun set over the ocean, or nearby Lana'i in the winter.

21.6
1.7

Puamana Beach Park. Lahaina town begins just beyond here.

Alternate route

22.2
1.1

Alternate route: Turn makai here for the first exit into Lahaina. Front Street, at this point a sleepy drive lined with some very pleasant villas, continues along the coast all the way through Lahaina then rejoins the highway beyond a giant Safeway supermarket.

23.3
0.0

Intersection with Lahainaluna Street. A left turn here brings you into the center of town. Two blocks down you pass a good natural food store and Fun Bike Rentals bicycle shop. Amidst their stable of solid mountain bikes they have several road bikes for rent, including a sweet little Tomasini. Yikes!

Two more blocks brings you to Front Street. The ferry and excursion boat marina is to your left here just a few blocks.

Kahului Airport—Wailuku-Iao Valley—Lahaina Bound

This route exposes you to the wide spectrum of the faces that are Hawaii. Less than one mile from the busy Kahului Airport you stop at beautiful Kanaha Beach Park, currently slated for expansion to include a campground. After paralleling a wildlife refuge for 2 miles you're suddenly dumped in the middle of industrial, downtown Kahului.

Next, you climb a busy Highway connecting Kahului with Wailuku, which is the county seat. Wailuku is home to county and state offices issuing camping permits as well as the only hostel on this part of the island.

Just as suddenly as the urban area began, it ends as you wind up the Iao Valley. Soon you are surrounded by lush tropical forest with a river rushing along the base of towering, green cliffs. The heat and humidity may seem overwhelming. Go slow, enjoy this beautiful place.

Rolling back out of spectacular Iao Valley, the Highway turns south and skirts the west Maui mountains below new subdivisions and golf courses as you cross the pineapple-covered central Maui isthmus. As you begin to drop gently back to sea level, small Kahoolawe Island comes into view beyond Ma'alaea Bay, a favorite haunt for wintering humpback whales.

Before long, this often wind-assisted glide brings you to the junction with Highways 380 and 30. The remaining trip to Lahaina is detailed in the Kahului-Lahaina route.

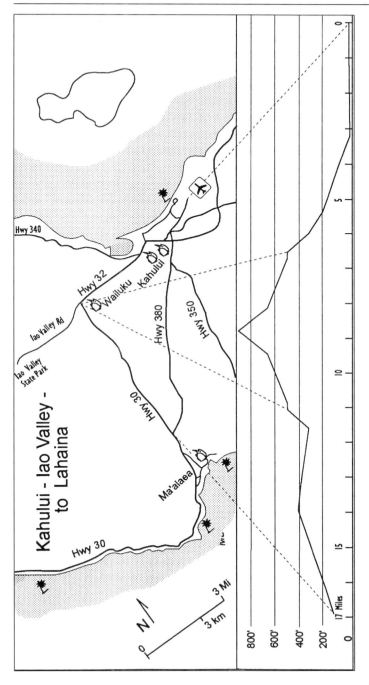

Kahului - Iao Valley - to Lahaina

Hwy 340

Hwy 32

Iao Valley Rd

Iao Valley State Park

Wailuku

Kahului

Hwy 380

Hwy 350

Hwy 30

Hwy 30

Ma'alaea

N

3 Mi

3 km

0

800'
600'
400'
200'
0

0
5
10
15
17 Miles

Miles from	*Miles from*
Kahului	*Lahaina*
0.0	*33.0*

Begin on Keoani Place in front of the baggage claim area near the rental car desks. There is plenty of area here to reassemble your bicycle.

0.3
32.7
Turn right off Keoani onto Ka'a Road following the signs to "Car Rental Agencies." Smile as you speed past the frenzied and tired auto tourists waiting in line for their cars, and head for the beach.

0.6
32.4
Turn right on Alahao Street. For the next 0.5 miles there are numerous access drives to Kanaha Beach Park which provides picnic tables, drinking water, and outdoor showers. It is also a great place to take your first, or last, dip in the ocean. A less-than-inspirational view of industrial Wailuku frames the view up the Iao Valley State Park as it cuts deeply into the razor-backed west Maui mountains. At press time, camping was not allowed at Kanaha Park. However, the State is planning to open the area to camping soon.

When you're ready to leave this first taste of paradise, return the way you came to the intersection of Ka'a and Alahao Roads. Continue straight here as Alahao becomes Amala Street. The wildlands to your left for the next 1.9 miles are a wildlife sanctuary and numerous species of tropical coastal birds can be seen.

3.0
30.0
Just prior to the first noisy industrial facility is a wholesale produce operation with a retail stand on the left. The prices and freshness are good here, however, several supermarkets also await ahead.

3.3
29.7
Go left on Hobron Street.

4.0
29.0
Turn right on busy Kaahumanu Street (Highway 36). This is the worst traffic you are likely to encounter in all of Maui.

4.5
28.5
Pass Kaahumanu Mall with its white canvas roof. This is a large new mall with lots of stores and eateries as well as a multiplex theater in case you

forgot to pack an essential or two. There is a Foodland supermarket on Kane Street just beyond the Sears Store. Beyond the mall, climb a short hill up to Wailuku. 0.5 miles ahead on your right is the Wailuku War Memorial Center where camping permits for the island Maui can be obtained.

6.0
27.0
Intersection with High Street. To the left are numerous government offices including those housing the administration of State Parks in case you still need to make arrangements for camping. To the right two blocks before High Street (Highway 30) is Market Street which sports a camping supply store and the Banana Bungalow Hostel. The supermarket here is the last one passed on this route until Lahaina, although several other smaller markets are passed beyond Wailuku.

Follow the signs up the hill to Iao Valley. Local traffic thins considerably from here to the end of the road.

6.2
26.8
The Bailey Family House Museum is to the right here. It's a good excuse to take a break from the climb and the heat and see a little of plantation-era Hawaii.

6.6
26.4
The hill thankfully levels off for 0.25 miles as you pass small fruit stands in front of some semi-palatial homes nestled in the thickening tropical forest. Listen for Iao stream running along side the road.

8.1
24.9
Sure the climb is fun—especially if you had the forethought to setup your wind trainer in a sauna—but check this out anyway. It's the Hawaiian Heritage Gardens where structures from eight different cultures important to the development of modern Hawaii are beautifully presented. There's fresh water in the spigots by the picnic area shelters to replace all the water your body is losing.

8.9
24.1
You've made it to the top. The Iao Valley parking lot at 880 feet affords views of the Iao Needle, a beautiful tropical forest and stream, and the central Maui plain below. Several short trails lead through the park from here. The intersection with High Street lays a blissful 2.9 miles and 550 feet below you.

11.7
21.3
Back in town and invigorated from the glide downhill. Turn right on High Street (Highway 30). The next 2.5 miles gently climb 80 feet in eleva-

tion. If the Trade winds are blowing you won't notice the grade, if the Trades are blowing hard, you'll have to use your brakes to keep it under 20 mph.

13.9
19.1
Pass through tiny Wiakapu with a market and intersection with Highway 305. Highway 305 is a cane-haul road. It is a marked intersection, but a very bad road.

14.8
18.2
On the hillside to the right is a huge home designed by Frank Lloyd Wright which vaguely resembles the latest version of the Starship Enterprise.

16.8
16.2
Junction with Highway 380, the short route to the Kahului Airport (6 miles away) is to your left. The road to fabled Lahaina lies to your right. Pick up remaining directions from the Kahului Airport-Lahaina: the Short Route tour at mile 7.2.

Lahaina—Kahului

Until recently, traveling this portion of the circuit around west Maui was restricted to folks with sturdy vehicles, nerves of steel, and all afternoon to spend due to a long and winding stretch of unpaved road. However, since the paving was completed a few years ago, the word is slowly spreading about the raw beauty of this portion of the island, and tourist traffic is slowly increasing.

The first eight level miles of this ride takes you past the purely resort towns along the Ka'anapali coast. But soon after passing through the largely residential town of Napili, the road narrows and the cycling becomes interesting to say the least.

Over the following 14 miles the road drops in and out of gullies carved by mountain streams reaching for the sea. The vegetation changes from pineapple and ironwood pines to dry pasture with patches of forest near the wetter gullies. Below the highway stretch beaches and wild lava shores.

Beginning in charming little Kahakuloa, where traditional lifestyles are pursued by the native residents, the newly paved one lane country road spends the next six pasture-lined miles climbing over a 1000-foot shoulder of west Maui and then drops down to Wailuku-Kahului.

Beyond Napili services are somewhat uncertain so stock up on supplies there. Fleming Beach Park at the bottom of the hill beyond Napili is a fine place to fill water bottles and relax before moving on down the coast.

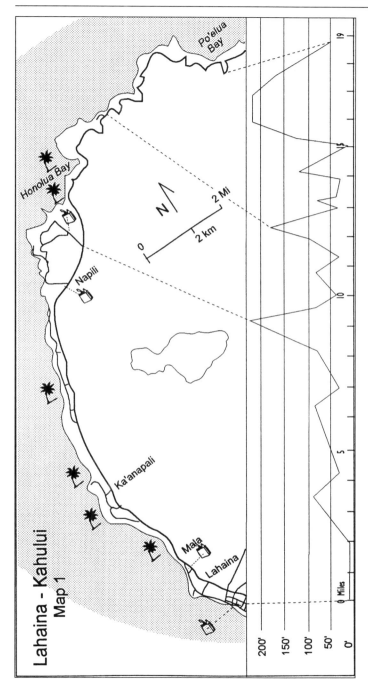

Lahaina - Kahului
Map 1

Po'elua Bay

Honolua Bay

Napili

Ka'anapali

Mala

Lahaina

N

0   2 km
      2 Mi

200'
150'
100'
50'
0'

0 Miles

5

10

15

19

41

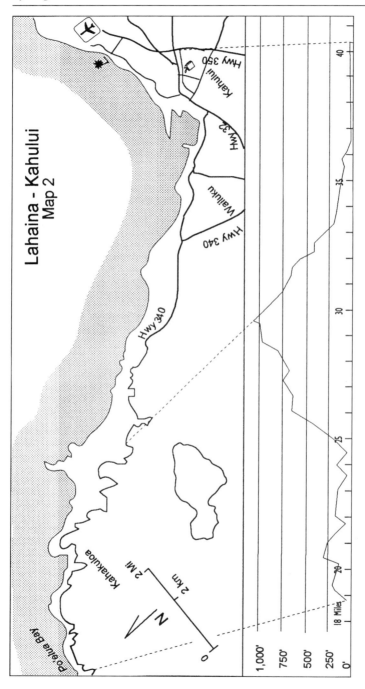

Miles from   *Miles from*
Lahaina   *Kahului*
0.0   *40.4*

Begin on Front Street at the Lahaina Wharf. Head North (Island Lana'i should be on your left).

0.7
39.7

Cultural site: For an interesting detour, a hard left at a sign to Mala Wharf near a small park takes you to the Jodo Mission at #12 Ala Moana Street. The mission features a beautiful large bronze Buddha backed by the west Maui mountains, a pagoda temple, and a monumental bronze bell which you can respectfully chime. Its vibration seems to go on forever.

1.0
39.4

Groceries: A really big Safeway Supermarket is on your right here. Stock up for the day's ride.

1.5
38.9

Turn left where Front Street rejoins Honoapiilani Highway 30, with its wide, officially designated bike lane along the shoulder.

2.1
37.3

Beach access and restrooms: A protected *makai* turn allows you to visit Wahikali State Park. Water, restrooms, and picnicking are available in the overused roadside park.

2.6
37.3

Hanakoo Beach Park access: This is the beginning of famous Ka'anapali Beach. It's a good place to check out team canoeing or just hang out on the beach for a while.

3.2
37.2

First exit to the hotels of Ka'anapali. This drive passes several grand resort hotels which can be fun to just cruise through, as well as several public beach access points. There is a pleasant paved walk stretching the length of the beach with numerous showers along the way making a cool ocean swim highly practical for the over-heated cyclist. There appears to be a low riff-raff factor here, but lock your bike to a palm tree anyway.

You can continue on along this busy looping road until it rejoins the highway, however, it is very busy and nearly shoulderless.

6.5
33.9
Ka'anapali Airport is *mauka*.

6.6
33.8
Pass over the top of a small hill affording tantalizing views of east Moloka'i, just 6 miles across a narrow strait.

7.1
33.3
Laundromat: Kahana Gateway Mall. There is a rare Laundromat here if in need.

8.0
32.4
Continuing straight begin climbing a small hill that can seem like a big hill if the Trades are blowing against you.

8.4
32.0
A confusing Bike Route sign would have you turn left here. This is an alternate route which leads you back down to sea level again only to climb back up to meet the highway at the top of a 250-foot hill.

On the other hand, the Napili shopping center at this intersection features a good supermarket and a really fine coffee-espresso bar. This is the last market until Lihui, 30 long miles away.

9.4
30.0
Beach and water access: Top of the hill followed by a Trade wind-defying descent at Fleming Beach Park, site of a fine sand beach, outdoor showers, restrooms, and some fairly snooty beach patrons. This is the last available drinking water for 30 miles.

10.4
29.0
End of the official Bike Route as shoulders narrow and traffic thins considerably.

10.5 + 11.5
28.5 + 27.9
Snorkeling: Two separate trails lead to Honolua Bay beaches. These two unimproved sites border a marine wildlife refuge which sport some of the best snorkeling I've ever enjoyed. No showers, no drinking water. I bring a 1.5 liter bottle of fresh water with me from

Fleming Beach to rinse off with. On your way up out of Honolua Bay be certain to stop and enjoy the viewpoints high above the sea. After you climb up out of Honolua Bay enter a brief table land. Welcome to Pineapple Land. Those huge trucks cruising by can smell awfully good if you like the spiky fruit. More great views of Moloka'i through the fragrant weeping pines.

The ride becomes vigorous over the next 20 miles as the Highway dips down into gulleys and back up onto headlands of ever-increasing size.

13.6
26.8
Surf access: Access road to a scenic and isolated beach. Make it your own for an hour. Remember to look behind you for wonderful views of Moloka'i.

13.9
26.5
Milepost 35 is followed by a pleasant drop into a beautiful little cove.

15.3
25.1
WARNING. STEEP GRADE AHEAD. So you think Law School looks tough, huh? Wait until you try to ride up the next 0.25 miles. The paved road is so steep that rear tires spin and slip on any bit of loose gravel. Never be embarrassed to walk your bike. You'll look even more foolish with a blown knee.

16.0
24.4
Congratulations, you've topped another hill!

16.5
23.9
A vicious cattle guard will rattle the frame and flatten the wheels of the intemperate cyclist.

16.8
23.6
A very cool shelf of exposed basaltic pillow lavas. Initially extruded underwater where the lava cools so rapidly that it forms pillow shaped globs. In the distance ahead, the Paia coast of east Maui at the foot of 10,000 feet Haleakala is visible for the first time.

18.8
21.6

Milepost 40.
20.9
19.5
The sign says "End State Highway" and the road surface shortly goes to pot. Fortunately, it remains bad for a very short time.

22.1
18.3
Smooth new pavement begins in the form of a one-lane country road.

23.6
16.8
Pass over a final headland before descending into the beautiful isolated town of Kahakuloa where a quaint old mission style church frames the view of the 630 feet monolithic Kahakaloa Head flanked by nearby flowering trees and palms. Aside from refreshing the soul, Kahakuloa also provides refreshment for the body in the form of two intermittently open roadside snack stands; one before and above town upon a scenic bluff, and another just before the bridge in town. Both are likely to be staffed by at least two charming young entrepreneurs and their friends on roller blades. No other services are available here.

24.5
15.9
Cross the bridge past the center of town at 40 feet elevation and begin a long, picturesque 1,000 feet climb through alternating pasture and forest. Except for the steep first 0.25 miles, the grade is consistent and reasonable.

26.2
14.2
Kalikiui Ranch—gifts and refreshments . . . why not rest a spell?

26.8
13.6
Milepost 12. 600 feet above sea level.

28.8
11.6
Milepost 10. 900 feet above sea level.

29.1
11.3
A locally owned fruit stand here can provide some welcome energy. The grade eases for the last 0.5 miles to the top of the hill.

29.7
10.7
Top of the hill at 1,020 feet. Milepost 9 is just ahead. Begin the long roll down to Wailuku. Use caution on the sharp, corners ahead. Remember, those are tourists driving those oncoming cars.

31.6
8.8
If going towards Wailuku the highway recommences as a well paved, two-lane road. Be wary of loose stone on these very tight corners over the next 4.5 miles.

[If traveling in the other direction to Lahaina, there are several signs posted at this point warning you off this route. Laugh at them and press on.]

36.1
4.3
Junction with Highway 340. If you are going to Wailuku or Lahaina, stay straight here on Highway 330 (Kahehili Road). Otherwise turn left onto Highway 340 to go to Kahului, the airport, Hana, Kihei, or the Haleakala.

Highway 340 becomes a very busy and congested road, however, the shoulder remains wide and traffic safely slow.

38.7
1.7
Intersect Highway 32, Kaahumanu Road. Stay straight here across Kaahumanu onto Kane Street.

39.0
1.4
Pass the Mall and a Foodland Market, then turn left on Kamehameha Avenue which soon sprouts a bike route.

39.6
0.8
0.6 miles on Kamehameha brings you past several fast food outlets and a large Safeway and takes you to Alamaha Street. Turn right on Alamaha.

40.3
0.1
0.7 miles down Alamaha Street brings you to Dairy Road. Turn left here.

40.4
0.0
0.1 miles on Dairy Road brings you back to the Island's main intersection; Highway 36 to Paia, Hana, and the upcountry is to the right here.

Kahului—Kihei—La Perouse Bay

The charms of majestic Makena Beach, neighboring clothing-optional "Little Beach," and the fantastic snorkeling around the Ahihi-Kina'u Natural Area Reserve around La Perouse Bay are powerful lures. Furthermore, the nearby resorts provide many of the amenities you might hope to enjoy during a Hawaii vacation. Restaurants, resort pools, night clubs, and cheap drink specials all abound in Kihei.

A visit to Makena Beach—La Perouse is somewhat problematic in terms of low cost accommodations. It is a 58-mile round trip from Baldwin Beach Park and a 56-mile round trip from Camp Pecosa near Lahaina, the two closest campgrounds. As alternatives there are several waterless wild camps near the end of this route and there are some rooms available in sunny Kihei in the $45 range.

The route begins at the southeast corner of Kahului and follows the lowest of the three highways traversing central Maui. As you approach Ma'alaea Bay, you can turn onto the 7-mile long designated bike path on the shoulder of Highway 31 as it curves above congested Kihei.

When the highway ends, drop down to curvaceous Wailea Alanui Road which winds down to the lava encrusted shoreline beyond Makena Beach and crosses one of the most recent lava flows on Maui to La Perouse Bay.

On the return trip you can avoid backtracking by staying low on South Kihei Road, a little bit of Los Angeles in Hawaii. Kihei offers services, but it also offers urban sprawl, traffic, and angry natives. It is an interesting place to say the least.

The Alternate South Kihei Road Route describes the path through to Highway 30 for those wishing to go on towards Lahaina.

Miles from Kahului	*Miles from LaPerouse*
0.0	*22.6*

Begin at the intersection of Highways 36 and 380 in Kahului. Follow directional signs to Kihei as you begin down Highway 380.

0.8
21.8
Approach a large intersection with Highway 350. Get in the left turn lane here and turn left, again following signs to Kihei. The next 0.5 miles of road is canopied by beautiful trees and, unfortunately, blighted by a huge sugar refining factory and the scream of jets landing at busy Kahului Airport.

1.4
21.2
Bear right here on Highway 350 as busy Hansen Road joins the highway near the smoking stacks of the sugar mill. A sugar museum is available 0.1 miles to the left down Hansen Road for the curious.

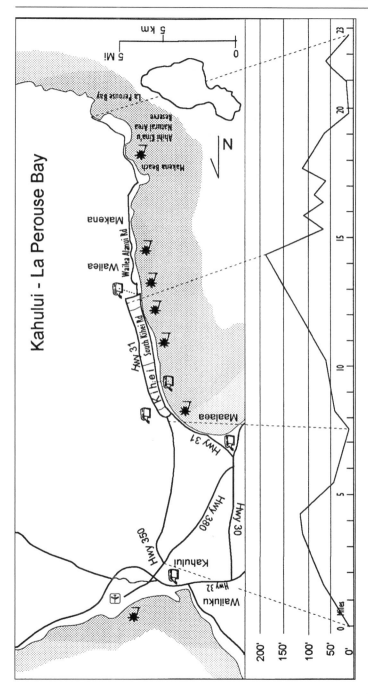

Kahului - La Perouse Bay

1.7
20.9
Continue a very gradual climb for the next 2.4 miles. If the trade winds are blowing, this bit of road takes you directly downwind where cruising at 25 miles per hour is nearly effortless. Remember the sensation on the return trip as you struggle upwind.

4.1
18.5
Cross the hump of the central Maui isthmus at 116 feet and drop gradually downhill to Ma'alaea Bay.

7.4
15.2
Junction of Highways 30 and 31. Turn south (left) on Highway 30 to begin the Kihei-Wailea "Bike Path," a wide, 7.3-mile long, well-paved shoulder on Highway 30. This makes a good express route around the congested and often hostile environment South Kihei Road presents to the through-riding cyclist.

8.3
14.3
Kihei Gateway Mall to the left. A convenience market here makes a good stop for some light grocery shopping. This is the last grocery you'll pass without dropping down onto South Kihei Road which has several adjacent supermarkets.

10.2
12.4
Lipon Road crossing. A *makai* (seaward) turn here brings you into "downtown" Kihei, site of restaurants, supermarkets, strip malls, public beaches, and sweaty tourists having fun American style.

13.4
9.2
If you want to visit Kihei, a *makai* turn here brings you to the southern terminus of South Kihei Road which flows through the center of town. See Alternative Return Route for a description of Kihei town.

14.7
7.9
240-foot elevation. In 1996 this is where the Highway and the bike path ends. However, new roadbed is being cleared to extend the Highway further south. Turn right and stop at the small park with a kiosk complete with a cool area map and a great view of Ma'alaea Bay and west Maui beyond. Lana'i island lies across a short channel to the left.

Glide down 0.6 miles to the shopping mall.

15.3
7.3
Turn left at this T intersection with Wailea Ananui Road toward Wailea-Makena and roll up and down and up and down and up and down over the "charming" hills of this charmingly planned resort. Beach accesses in this stretch usually feature restrooms, good water, and outdoor showers which are great to rinse off salt water after a dip in the ever-inviting ocean.

Many of the resorts that you pass over the next three miles make fascinating walking tours with grandiose architecture and formal gardens.

18.0
4.6
Many maps of Maui show a road beginning here and leading up to Ulupalakua Ranch on Highway 31. It has been closed and reclaimed by the Ranch. Non-employees are vigorously unwanted. Wailea-Ananui Road becomes Matiena Road here.

19.1
3.5
A snack van with cold drinks and shaved ice is usually here offering a truly welcome service on a hot dry day.

19.3
3.3
The cursed rolling hills end here at the turn off to Makena Beach Park. There are minimal facilities available here in the form of two chemical toilets—no drinking water. In the parking lot, lock your bike frame to something permanent and don't leave any removable valuables on your bike. Makena Beach is a wide strand of beautiful white sand with a vigorously playful surf. Ask the lifeguard if concerned about swimming safety.

Little Beach, a clothing-optional crescent of sand, lays beyond the rocky bluff at the north end of Makena Beach just beyond the lifeguard tower. Follow the stream of people over the narrow trail which climbs the low shoulder of a red cinder cone. The surf is a little more friendly here for the novice body surfer.

19.9
2.7
The pavement deteriorates here and the road goes to one lane as it winds along the low, lava lined coast. Views of the unimaginably blue shallows of Ahihi-Kina'u Natural Area Reserve are breathtaking. Beyond the private manor houses are several sites where folks have obviously been wild camping. You probably can too; no facilities though.

20.8
1.8
Begin to traverse 1.8 miles of a relatively recent lava flow. This is an extremely hot, dry area. Ulupalakua Ranch and Kanaio Homestead Village are visible on the mountain above.

22.6
0.0
End of the road. There are several additional dry camping spots nestled among the trees in this wildly beautiful area. Several different hikes extend beyond this point, the longest is the ancient paved foot trail which extends over ten miles south towards Kipahulu and connects with Highway 31 where it begins its climb up to Ulupalakua. The Ulupalakua Ranch foreman told me that he had seen mountain bikers riding this stretch of trail. Don't try it without a spare tire, and don't try it with packs. In fact, I wouldn't try it at all.

Alternate return route

From the end of the road at LaPerouse Bay return on the same route 7.3 miles to the T intersection leading up to Highway 31.

Alternate Route:
From Wailea-Alanui Road
From Junction Highways 31 & 30

0.0
10.4
Intersection in front of Wailea Shopping Center. Continue straight here.

0.6
9.8
Intersection with South Kihei Road. Turn left and glide down the hill into Kihei.

1.1
9.3
Beach parks line the left of the road and consumer services the right side of the road for the next 5.5 miles as the bike lane alternates between a marked path and a totally non-existent shoulder.

3.0
7.4
There is a laundromat in the strip mall on the *mauka* side (inland) at the 1800 block of South Kihei Road.

6.6
3.8
Turn right here for 0.1 miles to reach Highway 350 back to Kahului 7.4 miles away.

6.8
3.6
Junction with Highway 31. Lahaina is to the left on Highway 30.

Alternate return route cont.

10.4
0.0

Junction of Highway 31 with Honoapiilani Highway 30. Lahaina is 16 miles to the left (see Kahului—Lahaina route) and Wailuku is 5.1 miles to the right (see Kahului-Iao-Lahaina route).

Kahului—Haleakala

This 41-mile route, one way, includes three very different potential destination-stopping points and three different campgrounds so there is considerable leeway to plot your own itinerary.

The first 5 1/2 miles wends around the Kahului Airport then dips back to trace the boundary of the cane fields near the beach. Shortly before reaching Paia town you pass Baldwin Beach County Park where camping is allowed in an isolated field next to this very busy highway. If you're getting off a flight late in the day and need a place to crash, this is a welcome enough sight.

Paia town is a cross between Haight-Ashbury and Santa Fe on a small scale. Hippies swirl around the tourists stopped on their migration to Hana in this Old West-style town full of craft and jewelry shops. This a great place to stock up on groceries if you're staying at Rainbow County Park tonight.

Rainbow Park is three miles and 600 feet above Paia. This small Park is largely unimproved and is without water; however it does give you a little boost on your climb up the Haleakala and it is considerably more agreeable setting than Baldwin Beach Park. It is also only 4 miles and 1,000 feet below magical Makawao, the first destination on this leg.

Makawao is a working town. Its two biggest industries are cattle ranching and *woo woo* (i.e. your spiritual well being). Although I refrained from employing any of the plethora of Healing Artisans, there is something about the cooler mountain air and easy pace that make me feel just fine whenever I pass through town.

Because Makawao is less tourist oriented, prices on almost everything are lower here. There is a fantastic natural food store open at 8 A.M. seven days a week as well as several reasonably priced restaurants. If you're climbing to Hosmer Grove or beyond, this is a perfect place to stock up on vittles.

Another pretty perfect thing to do here is to visit Casanova's on the Southeast corner of the main intersection. Fine espressos and pastries can be enjoyed as you sit on the balcony and watch the world go by. The Courtyard Cafe two blocks down Baldwin Avenue makes an unforgettable Cinnamon Custard French Toast. Allow some time to browse the shops. This is a truly friendly place.

From Makawao you can follow Highways 400 then 37 for a pleasant tour through Maui's upcountry (Oheo-Kahului Tour), turn down Highway 365 and continue on to Hana (Haleakala-Hana Tour), or continue

up quiet Olinda and Hanamu Roads to Highway 377 and on to the summit of the Haleakala.

If choosing the later, BRAVO. Hosmer Grove Campground
awaits beyond a well-graded 7 mile southern traverse on Highway 377
specially equipped with wide shoulders expressly for bicycle traffic.
Use them. This is followed by 10 miles of nearly constant switchbacks
on Highway 378 where the grade is also very consistent. Find a good
gear and pace and stay with it. Hosmer Grove is 5,200 vertical feet
above Makawao. If you can do this portion in less than 4 hours, you're
a monster. If you can do it in 5 hours you're doing just fine. If you
need to take a rest, pretend you are taking a picture. If you're walking
your bike, you need better gearing.

As you climb higher you may notice that the air is cooler and drier, both
are welcome phenomenon on this monumental climb. Hosmer Grove will
likely be at least 20 degrees cooler than beach-side temperatures. Bring warm
clothes and sleeping gear to be comfortable up here.

Hosmer Grove itself was an attempt to find commercially marketable
timber species. Over 20 different types of foreign trees were planted (introduced) in this area. The result is a cool arboretum with a great self-guided nature trail and highly varied habitat for birds.

The Campground is first come-first served with a mythical limit of 25
campers. The truth is that the rangers don't care. There are no showers here,
but a refreshingly frigid sponge bath can be effected at one of the stand pipes.

Above Hosmer Grove the Highway winds back and forth another 10
miles and 3,200 vertical feet to the summit. The shoulder on Highway 378
is rather narrow, but traffic is slow and not heavy. It is especially light between sunrise, after the minions of tour buses have ascended with their
loads of bleary-eyed guests, and about 9:00 A.M. when the less ambitious
begin to arrive.

The air gets thin at this altitude so go slow, use your low gears, alternate
by standing up and pedaling occasionally. Remember that most folks can
pedal in a higher gear standing up. Try shifting up before you stand. Hope-
fully you've had the sense to shed your packs at the lowest possible altitude
to make this ride all the easier (no one's going to call you a sissy).

The views from the top are heavenly. In contrast to the smooth west side
of the mountain which you've been climbing, the east side of the summit
ridge drops away precipitously into a freshly laid mosaic of multi-colored volcanic cones and flows.

For me, the views pale in contrast with the exaltation I feel at having
completed this outrageous ascent. If you should just plain poop out on the
way up, don't lose heart, try to hitch a ride. Your bruised dignity will be
quickly salved by the outrageous rush of flying back down from the 10,000-
foot summit. Kind of like a slow motion sky-dive as the lowlands rush inex-
orably toward you. Smile, smile, smile. Then come back down.

From Hosmer Grove, you can either return to Makawao, or by turning
left at the junction of highways 378 with 377, climb for 1 mile then drop

steeply for 2.2 miles to the junction with Highway 37 where another left turn will lead you to an idyllic tour of the uplands on the way to Tedeschi Winery; or continue on and begin a counterclockwise tour of east Maui (see the Oheo-Kahului route for details).

Allow 2 hours to Rainbow Park and at least an additional hour up to Makawao. Two hours minimum are required for the trip from Hosmer Grove to the summit and 1/2 hour to get back down to the Campground. The trip from Hosmer down to Makawao requires 1 hour minimum.

Miles from Kahului	*Miles from Haleakala Summit*
0.0	*40.9*

Begin at the intersection of Hana Highway 36 and Dairy Road (Highway 380). Head east or follow the signs to Hana.

2.0
38.9
Intersection with Haleakala Highway 37. The Haleakala Highway presents a well graded and more direct route to the summit, for those in a hurry to get to the summit. However, it is also boring and full of speeding cars spewing exhaust. Furthermore, there are no inexpensive accommodations between this point and Hosmer Grove, 6,800 feet above and 25 miles beyond. A description of this leg can be found in the last leg of the Oheo-Kahului route.

5.0
33.9
After traveling past the Airport, some very industrial cane fields, and Spreckelsville, arrive at Baldwin (no relation to the author, unfortunately) Beach County Park. There is camping here in a fenced area placed mystifyingly close to the highway. There is also a fine beach for sunning and swimming, clean restrooms, drinking water, and outdoor showers.

You can camp here with several apparently homeless residents or continue on to Rainbow County Park (see entry at mile 8.6 for description).

5.6
35.3
Arrive in Paia, a quaint little town with one foot charmingly planted in the sixties. Full services available, groceries, restaurants, bakeries, and a bike shop next to the Laundromat.

5.8
35.1
Intersection with Baldwin Avenue at the traffic light. Turn mauka (inland) here for an inauspicious beginning to your climb to the uplands.

55

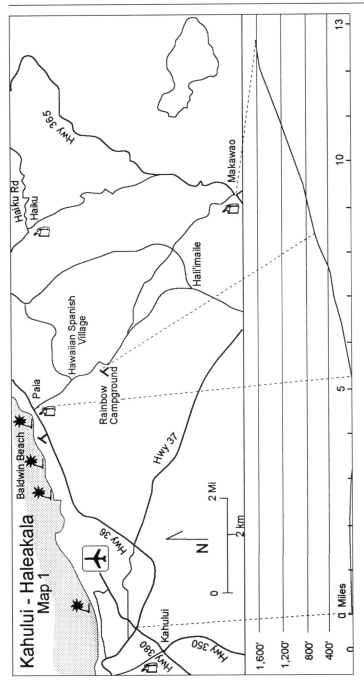

Kahului - Haleakala
Map 1

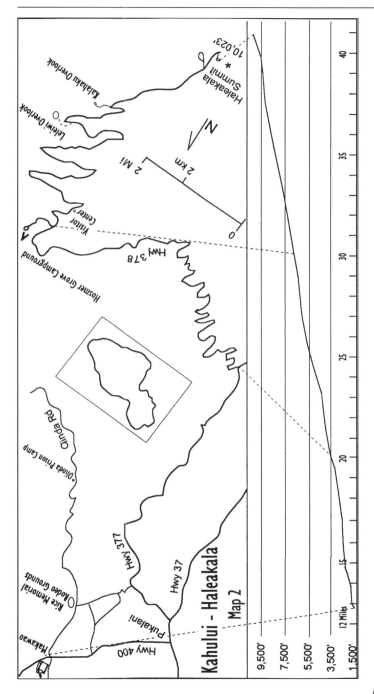

Kahului - Haleakala
Map 2

5.9
35.0
The Post Office and Mana Natural Food supermarket is on your left.

6.0
34.9
Paia Bike Shop and the Laundromat are on your left. You'll soon pass through Upper Paia and then an often-odoriferous sugar mill. Hard to believe they make something that tastes sweet here.

8.4
32.5
Makawao Union Church. This lovely stone and stained glass structure is your best water source for your stay at Rainbow County Park. There are numerous hose bibs as well as a drinking fountain, all with good water. I filled two large water bottles and used them to rinse off the road grime back at camp. You're at 600 feet here.

8.6
32.3
Rainbow Park. This facility is poorly marked and at first look you are likely only to see the neighboring farmer's KEEP OUT signs. The highway may seem busy here but it quiets down after 10 P.M. Your biggest nocturnal disturbance is likely to be late arriving tourists just off the 9:55 P.M. flight from Los Angeles, so camp up the hill away from the parking lot. The covered gazebo nestled in the ruins of a formal Japanese garden offers shelter from the frequent *mauka* (inland) showers. There are no showers here and no running water. The chemical toilets are well maintained.

9.5
31.4
Stay on Baldwin Avenue as you pass the turn-off to Maunaolu College and reform school as the quiet county road climbs above the coast through pineapple fields.

10.8
30.1
Continue straight through the intersection with Hali'imaile (NOT Hawaiian for Holy Moly) Road.

11.3
29.6
Point of Interest: Pass the turn to the Ulumalu Art Center. This thriving center and gallery is ensconced in a beautiful old plantation house with lovely formal gardens and a nifty view. Take the time for at least a quick visit to this friendly place.

12.1
28.8
Veteran's and Community cemeteries mark the outskirts of Makawao.

12.7
28.2
Intersection of Baldwin Avenue (Highway 390) and Highway 400. You've climbed to 1,610 feet above sea level. To the right here is access to Highways 37 and 377 through the upcountry. Left brings you back down towards the coast and the beginning of the amazingly scenic portion of the Hana Highway. To continue on to the Haleakala, go straight on Olinda Road.

12.7
28.2
The climb to Hosmer Grove begins anew at the intersection of Highways 400 and 390 (Olinda Road). At this intersection head up Olinda Road. The first 0.2 miles is the steepest grade on this whole route. Continue on Olinda for 1 mile as it winds though green pastures and eucalyptus groves.

13.7
27.2
Turn right on Hanamu Road at the Oskie Rice Memorial Rodeo Grounds.

14.4
26.5
Pass straight by a good road on the right headed down to residential Makawao and continue on up Hanamu Road as the road curves steeply up through a eucalyptus forest. You are likely to begin encountering groups of tourists in matching fuchsia or fluorescent yellow jumpsuits and motorcycle helmets "Riding the Volcano" as the ads say. They are on guided tours which begin at the summit. They paid at least $100 for the experience. Imagine how much more rich your journey will be.

14.8
26.1
The road forks as you approach Highway 377. Stay left here and begin a 4.9 mile, 1,400-foot climb on Highway 377. As is the case with most State Highways in Hawaii, this one features a well graded and consistent climbing angle. Find a low and comfortable gear and be patient. You've got 17 miles and 5,400 vertical feet to Hosmer Grove.

16.0
24.9
A short downhill, feels good.

16.2
24.7
2,500-foot elevation.

18.0
22.9
3,000-foot elevation.

19.0
23.9
Two restaurants in this area offer services (restrooms, food, and water) if you are in need.

19.7
23.2
Junction of Highways 377 and 378. A large wooden sign welcomes you to Haleakala National Park and points up the hill; follow Highway 378 up to the left.

Continuing straight on Highway 377 would bring you up a 400-foot, 1-mile climb followed by an exciting 2-mile descent to the junction with Highway 37 above Kula town. Route information from that point can be found at Mile 35.7 on the Oheo Gulch-Kahului route.

20.0
20.9
At the 3,500-foot level rejoice in the welcome sight of the Sunrise Protea Farm. The wonderful nursery offers cold drinks, snacks, water, picnicking, restrooms, gardens of Protea, and a great view of central and west Maui far below. If you have serious concerns about the weather, this is a good place to inquire about conditions above. It is not unusual at this height to be ensconced in a bank of clouds and yet have clear weather above.

21.7
19.2
4,000-foot elevation sign.

22.2
18.7
Enter a shady, fragrant eucalyptus grove. The Highway circles a beautiful horse ranch framed by a white rail fence. Trail rides are offered here. Watch for an amiable group of would-be *paniolos* (cowboys) who will likely cheer you on in your endeavor. This is the last significant stand of trees on the ascent. Enjoy their cool shade while it lasts.

You'll find that if you stop at any pull-out from this point onward, transient motorists will alternately offer words of amazed encouragement, and ask you questions only a seasoned tour guide could answer.

24.5
16.4
Pass the 5,000-foot marker near the Milepost 5 sign.

25.6
15.3
Milepost 6—you're at 5,400 feet now.
26.5
14.4
This is the last hairpin turn and the last of 23 switch-backs on this lower portion of Highway 378. A 2.5 mile long northeasterly traverse begins.

27.1
13.8
6,000-foot elevation. Only 800 vertical feet to the campground.

27.2
13.7
The grade levels refreshingly for 0.35 miles. Don't get cocky.

27.9
13.0
Gnarly cattle guard, use caution. Remember to watch for these guards on the way back down.

29.0
11.9
Another nasty cattle guard. Enter into an intermittent forest zone with welcome shade on a sunny day.

29.1
11.8
6,500-foot elevation.

29.8
11.1
Enter Haleakala National Park bounded by the last of the cattle guards. The pay station is 0.15 miles ahead. The fee for bicycles is $3 for a 5-day pass. This station is open only during normal business hours; however, out of deference for the hoards of pre-sunrise visitors, the gates never close. If you pass during non-office hours, simply ride on by.

30.1
10.8
The turn to Hosmer Grove Campground is to the left here. The campground is 0.7 miles down this access road. Cool water and shady

trees await weary cyclists. If Hosmer is your destination and you find yourself at the Visitors Center, STOP. Turn around and go back down 0.7 miles. Once at the campground stake out your campsite; it's first come, first served.

30.8
10.1
Continuing on up the mountain, pass the 7,000-foot elevation mark just before the Visitor Center. If you've just spent a chilly night at Hosmer Grove Campground, it's best to wait until sunrise to begin your ascent. Pre-dawn traffic is heavy, and it is really cold before sunrise. Besides, you miss the views. If possible, do get out of your tent when your neighbors start banging pots one hour before sunrise. The train of cars and buses climbing the hill above you present a beautiful display of lights.

For the next 2.0 miles the uphill grade eases relatively. Rest assured that it increases to match that of the lower portion of the climb soon enough.

30.9
10.0
Park Headquarters and Visitor Center. Here there are restrooms with hot and cold running water, telephones, and an interesting array of information about Haleakala National Park.

32.1
8.8
First hairpin turn as you begin the second of 8 switchbacks. The grade increases slightly here. Remember that you still have 9.7 miles and 2,800 feet of elevation to go in ever-thinning air. Set a conservative pace and expect the rest of the climb to take at least 1.5 hours of saddle time.

33.6
7.3
Here begins a slightly steeper, short straight centered on Milepost 14.

34.3
6.6
The fifth hairpin turn brings you up to 8,000 feet.

35.7
5.2
Milepost 16.

37.1
3.8
Parking lot for Leleiwi Overlook. This nearly level, five-minute hike takes you to a covered scenic overlook and a view that will take away what-

ever breath you have left. From here you get your first, and my favorite, view of Haleakala Crater with the big island Hawaii beyond. Look closely at the near vertical ridge to the left to pick out Halemau'u trail zig-zagging up a green cliff—Yikes! And hikers think we're crazy?

37.8
3.1
9,000-foot elevation.

38.5
2.4
This last hairpin turn, which is punctuated by the access road to Kalahaku Overlook, marks the beginning of a final 1.7-mile traverse to the summit. To your right Moloaka'i looms above and beyond the 5,000-foot high West Maui Mountains. Across a short strait to the left of West Maui lies Lani'a. Further to the left is desolate Kahoolawe, and just off the shore below you is tiny Molokini islet.

39.3
1.6
Ahead and to the left get a glimpse of Red Hill summit and the white telescope domes of Science City nearby. Watch for distinctive Silver Sword plants on the red lava hillside above you.

40.2
0.7
Turnoff to the Haleakala Overlook Visitors Center. This is a fine excuse to get out of the saddle and catch your breath for the steep, final 0.6-mile, 250-foot assault on the summit. There are restrooms here and some really nasty-tasting, but potable, water. There is a trail head leading down into the caldera floor beginning at this parking lot. If time and weather allow, the first mile or two of this hike is awe-inspiring. The barren multi-hued cinder slopes are punctuated with silver sword plants and geologically young volcanic domes. Far below you can see how the lava has flowed over the rim of the caldera into the rain forest below.

40.7
0.2
Continue past the turnoff to astronomical observatories which are closed to the public. Stay to the right here, just 0.16 miles to go.

40.9
0.0
Parking lot for the summit lookout at Red Hill, elevation 10,023 feet—Yahoo! Check out the view and savor your accomplishment. More than likely it will be cold on top so bundle up before you get chilled. The ride down

is long and requires very little physical exertion so it is easy to get really cold as you coast through the curves.

On your descent, be weary of cars, both oncoming and descending. Drivers are likely to be gawking at the scenery and not paying attention to details such as center lines and speeding bicyclists.

Kahului—Hana

The Hana Highway is legendary among those who have driven it, and it is the most enchanting road I have ever ridden. The first 13 miles take you around the broad northern foot of the Haleakala, through Paia with an atmosphere out of the 1960s, then past Hookipu Beach where some of the most serious wind surfers in the world hang out. Eighteen miles south of Kahului all local traffic stops as you enter the eastern tropical rain forest. Traffic slows to bicycle speed and smiling motorists shout encouragement. Every half mile presents you with another waterfall or headland view of the coastline and the ocean below. The forest is sprinkled with huge flowering African tulip trees, giant flame-blossomed ginger, groves of bamboo and more shades of green than one can imagine. The ride finishes with a seven-mile-long ride down to Wainapanapa State Park and peaceful Hana beyond. All in all, a slice of cycling heaven.

If it has been raining recently it is best to check road conditions on the Hana Highway. This part of the island is the wettest lowland area in all of Maui County and the highway is subject to temporary closure due to slides and wash-outs. Call the outdoor activity report at 877-5111 for the latest information.

The ride to Paia is nearly flat as you roll past the Airport and on to Baldwin Beach County Park with camping available. The wide highway shoulder narrows a few miles outside of Kahului and traffic stays heavy.

The shoulder disappears altogether 2.2 miles beyond Paia. This sometimes harrowing 7 mile portion is made more so by continued heavy commercial traffic and frequent head winds both of which abate soon after Highway 36 becomes scenic Highway 360 at the junction with Highway 365 down from Makawao.

An alternate detour through Haiku offers some relief from this unremarkable bit of road. Another option is to detour up through Makawao town. This route adds 3.5 miles and 1,000 vertical feet to the trip. On the other hand, you miss 10 miles of somewhat unpleasant highway and instead tour through wind-sheltered, cooler upland areas. Plus, you get to visit Makawao, one of my favorite places in the world. See the Kahului-Haleakala route introduction for a description of friendly Makawao.

To return to the Hana Highway from Makawao, turn southwest onto Highway 400 (Kaupakulua Road) at the junction in downtown Makawao. Stay on Highway 400 for 6.5 miles. You'll roll through quiet neighborhoods and drop 1,030 feet to the well-marked junction with Highway 36 which changes its designation to Highway 360 at the junction. Turn right to continue on to Hana Highway 360, left on Highway 36 to return to Kahului.

Twelve and one-half miles beyond Paia on Highway 36, which becomes Highway 360 (at the junction with Highway 400), the real Hana Highway begins. The next 28 miles of road is the most sublime bicycle ride I have ever experienced. For several miles the road dips and climbs out of waterfall-draped gullies with cool freshwater pools and tropical rain forests all around.

Beyond tradition-bent Keanae, the Highway climbs 1,200 feet into a banyan-sprinkled forest thick with the song of tropical birds. Finally you coast several miles down to the coastal plain and Wainapanapa State Park with da kine camping and State-owned cabins for rent to those who've planned several months ahead.

Several hundred sharp curves keep the tourists at a reasonable rate of speed and the atmosphere at rest stops is generally convivial. Who could be grumpy in this splendor?

Forty-two miles from Paia, Wainapanapa State Park offers camping, good water and restrooms, cabins, and some marvelous natural attractions. Wainapanapa Caves, at the north end of the campground, are cool, herb draped, fresh-water filled lava tubes. An ancient Hawaiian "paved" trail extends in both directions along this lava-edged coast. The trail to the south extends over two miles to Hana town through vibrant green ti trees growing on jet black lava washed by the iridescent blue sea. Just less than 1 mile from the campground the trail passes a well-preserved Heiau. It is traditional to wrap a stone in the long leaf of a nearby ti tree and leave it with a prayer as an offering: however, the authorities now feel that this practice is degrading the site, so leave your offering down the trail away from the Heiau itself.

Beyond the incomparable coast at Wainapanapa lies sleepy Hana, dominated by the Hana Maui Resort and bejeweled by several small beaches.

Miles from Kahului	*Miles from Hana*
0.0	*49.6*

Begin at the intersection of Hana Highway 36 and Dairy Road (Highway 380) in Kahului. Follow the signs to Hana to the east. For a description of the route up to Paia see the first leg of the Kahului-Haleakala route.

5.6
44.0
Paia town. This a great place to get supplies for the rest of your ride. There are several small stores on Highway 36 and the well stocked Mana Natural Food Store is on the right one block up Balwin Avenue.

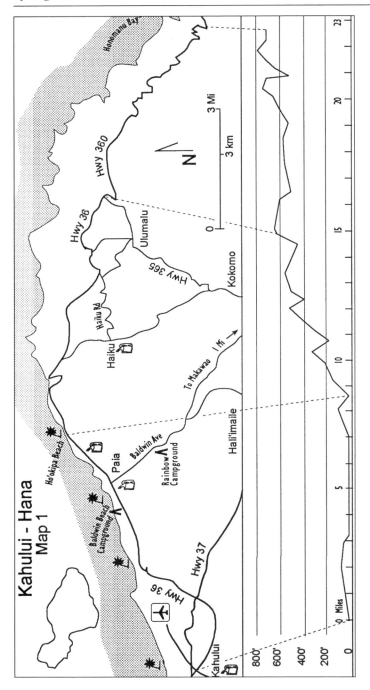

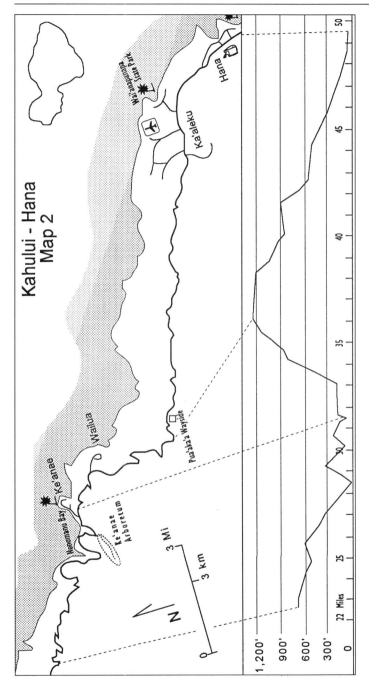

Kahului - Hana
Map 2

Alternate route: The upland route through Makawao discussed in the introduction to this section leaves the Hana Highway by taking a right at this point onto Baldwin Avenue at the traffic light. The 1,000-foot additional climb and extra 3.5 miles of riding is all on quiet winding roads. See the Kahului-Haleakala route for details of the ride up to Makawao and the descent back down to Highway 36-360. The Makawao alternate rejoins this route 9.5 miles ahead (15 miles from Kahului) and bypasses a long section of industrial-strength traffic on a narrow-shouldered Highway 36.

5.9
43.7
Kuau Community convenience store.

6.9
42.7
Beach access at Mama's Fish House. Not a casual diner.

7.8
41.8
Hookipu Beach Park. In addition to being a great spot to watch some world-class wind surfers kiting off big waves, this park also offers good water and dubious restrooms as well as outdoor showers. No camping, and swimming beyond the narrow reef is dangerous.

The Highway shoulder ends here and doesn't reappear for about 75 miles.

9.9
39.7
Haiku Alternate Route
Milepost 11 coincides with the well-signed turn-off to Haiku town on Haiku Road. If the traffic or the head winds have you unnerved, Haiku Road can offer refuge as an alternate route. However it does add 1.9 miles to your ride. A description of this route follows.

Alternate route

0.0
4.2
This short detour leads you off busy Highway 36 and through quiet forested roads and homes. Turn right onto Haiku Road at Milepost 11. The first 0.8 miles of the hill is a little steep as you begin to climb 300 vertical feet to Haiku, 1.6 miles ahead.

1.2
3.0
Major intersection. Bear right and stay on Haiku Road.

Alternate route cont.

1.6
2.6
Downtown Haiku. This immediate area features a supermarket, a natural food store, a natural food take out window, a post office, and an organic peanut wholesale outlet. Chow down.

Turn left at the intersection to stay on Haiku Road. Going straight here puts you on Kokomo Road.

2.8
1.4
Descend into an especially pretty gully lined with African tulip trees.

3.3
0.9
An especially confusing intersection. Stay on Haiku Road, the only two alternatives without stop signs.

4.2
0.0
End alternate route. Re-enter the Hana Highway 36 at 12.3 miles from Kahului on the primary route description.

9.9
39.7
Milepost 11 on the Hana Highway.
12.3
37.3
Reconnection of Haiku alternate route. Haiku Road rejoins Highway 36 from the right.
12.4
37.2
Top of this climb at 503 feet. Over the next 2.7 miles the Highway rolls up and down nearly continuously but gains only 100 feet.
12.9
36.7
Milepost 14.

13.4
36.2
Continue stright at the intersection with Ulumalu Road followed by the driveway to the Maui Grown Market and Deli. This is the last chance for food of any sort until the Halfway-to-Hana Snack Bar 18.9 miles ahead.

14.7
34.9
Ride straight through the intersection with Holokai Road.

14.9
34.7
Milepost 16.

15.0
34.5
Reconnection of Makawao alternate route.

Intersection with Kaupakulua Road (Highway 400) to Makawao. The Hana Highway changes designation from Highway 36 to 360. The character of the land changes to tropical forest here, and the road becomes slow (for cars) and winding. Over the next 13.5 miles the Highway repeatedly dips down into refreshing stream-filled gullies and climbs back up to view forest-studded ridges. Be wary of tourists trying to have a really fast vacation, and be prepared to accept the accolades of the more appreciative motorists. Locals seem especially receptive to cyclists on this road.

18.0
31.6
The gullies begin in earnest.

21.2
28.4
The uphill ravine *mauka* is filled with an otherworldly bamboo forest. Rain forest dominates the land for several miles from here.

22.0
27.6
At 780 feet this is the high point on the highway between Paia and Keanae.

25.9
23.7
This is one of the most picturesque streams along the Hana Highway. Take the time to walk the short path to a view above the falls. Go for a swim. Beware of EXTREMELY slick rocks. What a beautiful place our world is.

27.1
22.5
Kaumahina State Wayside. Bodacious restrooms and water here and an inspirational view of the Keanae Peninsula ahead. This is the last completely reliable water stop until Wainapanapa State Park, 20 miles ahead.

28.8
20.8
Milepost 14. Access to Honomanu Bay featuring a good beach, swimming, and a lot of informal camping. No fresh water available here.

29.3
20.3
The top of a 320-foot climb out of Honomanu Bay.

31.2
18.4
YMCA Camp Keanae. This organizational camp requires reservations. See "Where to Stay" for complete information.

31.4
18.2
Keanae Arboretum. This lush and fragrant paved walk is an excellent opportunity to learn the names of some of the vegetation you've been enjoying.

31.5
17.1
Side Trip: Keanae town turn-off. A short steep hill takes you down into the closest thing you're likely to find to authentic Hawaiiana outside of Nihau, the exclusively Native Hawaiian island. This is not a tourist attraction. This is a group of Hawaiians trying to reconstruct a nearly extinct lifestyle. You may not feel welcome here; however, if you act respectfully you will be tolerated. You will also be treated to a close-up view of traditional agriculture with lovely fields of taro lined by bananas, mango, guava, and other plants. This is a lovely, inspiring place.

31.9
16.7
A wonderful overlook of the scenic taro and banana fields of Keanae below.

32.3
17.3
It's the Halfway-to-Hana Refreshment Stand.
Snacks and cold drinks prepare you for the 1,100-foot climb up to Pua Kaa State Park 5.2 miles ahead.

32.8
16.8
Just past Milepost 18 be on the look-out for an especially aggressive little terrier. Yikes!

33.7
15.9
Wailua Valley State Park. A short walk inland reveals a commanding view of *mauka* Wailua. 500-foot elevation.

35.8
13.8
Just before Milepost 21 cross a bridge with a large pool to the right and a really high waterfall drops precipitously below the road to the left. You've climbed to 1200 feet in elevation.

36.1
13.5
At 1280 feet, you're at the top. It's nearly all down hill to Wainapanapa Park from here.

37.5
12.1
Pua Kaa State Park. No water and some really ghastly restrooms. The picnic area is lovely though, with prehistoric-looking fern trees and red-tinged giant ginger plants. The bright orange blossoms of the ubiquitous African orchid trees often litter the road. There is a cool fresh-water pool suitable for the determined swimmer here.
Roll downhill for the next 8 miles as the tropical rain forest turns slightly drier and collapses under the onslaught of grazing cattle and sheep.

41.4
8.2
A sleepy fruit stand with a decidedly unambitious proprietor.

42.1
7.5
The dominance of scrub land heralds the coming long descent.

45.7
3.9
At the foot of the descent on your right is Hana Gardenlands, not just another nursery! Pull in here and treat yourself to a fine little arts and crafts gallery and a lunch counter serving fresh, whole foods, salads, cool drinks, and really good iced espressos. A welcome taste of civilization.

46.8
2.8
Camping: A large sign announces the turn-off to Wainapanapa State Park and Campground just past Milepost 32. The road down to the park is about 0.7 miles long. If it's getting late in the afternoon and you need supplies, consider

cruising the 2.8 miles into Hana's Hasegawa General Store which is not known for its late hours (closes at 3:30 on Sundays). It's the only grocery store for miles.

47.4
2.2
The Hana Elementary School.

48.5
1.1
Hana Hospital is on your right. Stay right on the main Highway through the following intersection for the most direct route through town.

See the Hana alternate route for a description of this makai road through lower Hana town.

48.9
0.7
Hana Maui Resort. Mucho expensivo y pretensioso. And luxurious. If you can get past the snooty doorman, the main facility makes a delightful stroll. No nasty restrooms here.

49.3
0.3
A *makai* turn on Hauoli Street takes you to the trail to the clothing-optional Red Sand Beach. See Hana alternate route for details (Mile 1.35).

49.6
0.0
To the left is Hasegawa General Store which has just about everything you really need. To the right, up the hill is the Hana Ranch variety store and restaurant in case you don't want to cook. Beware of restaurants with captive audiences.

Alternate route

Hana Alternate Route

0.0
At the intersection just beyond the hospital (48.6 miles from Kahului) turn left. This beautiful side road takes you past several overnight accommodations. Continue a 1.1 mile glide down to Hana Bay Beach Park whose white sand is flanked by a lava shelf and a black sand beach to the west and a dramatic cinder cone draped in weeping pines to the east. This working harbor offers swimming, sunning, and Tutu's snack bar. Ride out to the pier for a good view of Hana and the Haleakala above. Just above the entrance to the Park is the Hana Cultural Center and Museum.

Alternate route cont.

1.1

On the opposite side of the Harbor's cinder cone is the extremely beautiful, clothing-optional Red Sand Beach. To reach this treasure, continue along Uakea Road past the Harbor turnoff up a steep little hill.

1.35

In front of the Hana Community Center, Uakea Road intersects with Hauoli Road which leads shortly to the main Highway and the Hana Maui Resort. Lock your bike up at the Center and walk down to the end of Uakea Road where you'll find a parking lot for the Hotel Hana Maui. To the left and just outside the parking lot fence is the beginning of the five-minute trail to the beach. Footing is a little slick. To your right you can see the big island Hawaii in the distance. You may also notice strangely shaped blocks of concrete along the trail and the shore below. Look kind of like headstones, don't they? Guess what's eroding from the slope above you. Continue on the trail until you take a sharp left after a little hill. You'll know it when you see it. Swimming in the blue shallows of the tiny bay at Red Sand Beach is safe, however, stay well away from the currents around the breaches in the protective reef wall.

Hana—Oheo Gulch

Just past the last gas station in Hana you pass a sign which says "Haleakala National Park-Kipahulu District 9.3 Miles." Didn't think you were so close to the summit, did you? Well . . . you're not. Several years ago a team of naturalists hiked down the Oheo valley from the Haleakala summit caldera and discovered a completely untouched and little-altered valley supporting species thought long extinct. As quickly as possible the Park Service incorporated the Oheo valley into Haleakala Park and shut it off to all human contact save minimal study projects. King Kong has yet to be sighted, but you never know.

Beyond Hana, potable water becomes a logistical problem. Oheo Campground has no water available so you must either bring in all your water or buy it from the Park Headquarters at $.75 per half liter. Furthermore, with the exception of the sometimes-open Kaupo store, there is no water source over the next 27 miles beyond Oheo Gulch, and tomorrow's ride is through hot, dry desert. I recommend buying two or three 1.5 liter bottles of water at the store in Hana.

One additional water source is available past Hana. What a happy coincidence that it should be at Hamoa Beach, one of the prettiest beaches in all of Hawaii. See the alternate route to Hamoa at the end of this section for details.

Oheo Gulch National Park and Campground await you just 9 short roller coaster miles form Hana. The star of the Park is Oheo stream. A two-mile trail follows the stream uphill from the Visitors Center, past cool, inviting pools perfect for a quick swim, then passes through mysterious bamboo forests whose thick growth nearly blocks out the tropical sun, and ends at misty Wiamoku falls. Below the Highway, Oheo stream gathers in three successive pools adorned with a wreath of brightly colored tourists. These cool, fresh water pools are perfect for soaking away the grit of the day.

Miles from	*Miles from*
Hana	*Oheo*
0.0	*9.1*

From the Hasegawa General Store in Hana head south. Somewhere near here Hana Highway 360 becomes Piilani Highway 31. Hasegawa's is the only grocery stop today, so stock up.

0.1
9.0
Pass a sign that reads "Haleakala National Park Kipahulu District 9.3 miles."

0.7
8.4
Milepost 51.

1.2
7.9
Top of a small hill at 190 feet.

1.3
7.8
Alternate route: Access to Koki and Hamoa Beach begins to the left here. For details see Alternate Route-Hamoa Beach at the end of this leg. The Alternate adds only 0.3 miles to the trip, and potentially two or three extremely enjoyable hours.

2.5
6.6
Alternate route rejoins Pi'ilani Highway 31.

2.7
6.4
Milepost 49. The Highway becomes less traveled beyond Hana and hills and turns become less well engineered.

5.2
3.9
Begin the first of several short steep hills as the Highway again begins to dive in and out of gullies.

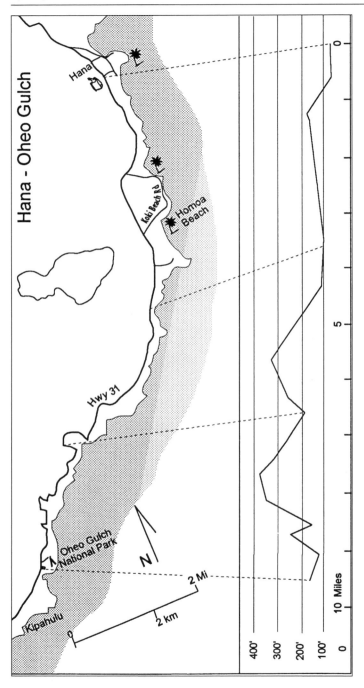

Hana - Oheo Gulch

6.6
2.5

This valley near Milepost 45 has three usually active waterfalls. The steep valley walls are densely populated with plants of countless shades of green.

7.7
1.4

For the next 0.5 miles pass a series of refreshing streams. Yum. Listen for native birds as you serenely glide through the dark tropical rain forest.

8.4
0.7

One last stream valley before gliding down into the Park.

8.5
0.6

Virgin Mary of the Rocks. Weird. You'll understand what I mean when you see it.

8.8
0.3

Cross Oheo Stream. Stop and look off the bridge towards the sea. I once watched a young man jump from this bridge into the pool below, then jump into the next pool, and finally jump into the last. You ever notice that only young people do such things, hmmm?

Enter the Haleakala National Park.

9.1
0.0

Turn off to the Park Headquarters. Save yourself the agony of an additional 0.1 mile of bad road and wait to take the second entrance into a large mowed field cum parking lot. Follow the signs down the steep unpaved road to the campground.

The large wide grassy field that is the apparent camping area is adequate with garbage cans, tables, and pretty OK chemical toilets. But wait, see those ti trees down by the ocean? Wouldn't that be a nice place to camp. Well, you're right. Go grab a shady, ocean-side site and trade the noise of late-arriving car campers for the gentle hiss of the sea.

Alternate route

Alternate route by Hamoa Beach.

Miles from Alternate Start	*Miles from Alternate Stop*
0.0	*1.5*

Alternate route cont.

At 1.35 miles from Hana turn left down the hill. The pavement here is pretty bad but lasts only for 1.1 miles.

0.4
1.1
Koki Beach Wayside at the bottom of the hill features views of iridescent blue waters crashing into lava sea arches scenically framed by windbent *kiawe* trees.

1.1
0.4
Watch for the stone wall and stairway to luxurious Hamoa Beach Park, one of the prettiest sunning and swimming beaches on Maui. Don't miss this one. There are extensive facilities for guests of local resorts, including a bar, but don't be dissuaded. This is a public beach. Thanks to the pleasant outdoor shower facility you can enjoy a cool dip or soak up some sun and then get cleaned up before resuming your ride to Oheo camp. This is also a fine place to fill any vacant water bottles you have. The next free water is 41.5 miles ahead in Keokea.

1.5
0.0
Rejoin Piilani Highway 31 now 2.5 miles from Hana.

Oheo Gulch—Kahului

In many ways this 52-mile route from Oheo Gulch to Kahului is the most challenging ride covered in this book. In a sense it is also one of the most gratifying, for having once met the various challenges it presents, you will know that you've achieved an impressive level of skill as a cyclist. This route begins in lush rain forest and slowly brings you into the severe dryness created by the Haleakala rain shadow. There is no tourist development on this western coast, only 25 miles of rugged coast, several thousand cows, you, and your thoughts. Near Keokea town the landscape becomes green and closely grazed with non-stop views of central Maui. Here also the pavement becomes excellent and services are available. The ride concludes with a 16-mile, 3,000-foot downhill roll into Kahului.

Before beginning this leg, check with the Haleakala Park Headquarters to make certain that the road is open. Heavy rains upslope often wash out, wash over, or otherwise close the Piilani Highway. To ride the 12 miles to Wailaulau Gulch and be turned back by high water might drive the weaker among us to madness.

This is an especially challenging tour, mentally as much as physically. Four miles beyond Oheo Gulch the Paved Highway turns to an often coarsely graveled, at times wash-boarded, single-lane dirt road. Going is so slow that

I have actually been attacked by mosquitoes while riding near Kaupo. This portion is often closed when rains upslope swell the intervening streams and the bridgeless road is inundated.

The good news is that thanks to recent road work, only 4 miles remain unpaved. Brevity helps make this 1-hour crawl bearable. Covering this section early in the day helps you miss the dust-generating tourist traffic and some of the heat. If you go very early in the morning, the Kaupo store will still be closed. However, the stores' erratic hours are a closely guarded family secret and its best not to plan on it being open. This rough first section of this ride takes you from rain forest to near desert scrublands before the pavement resumes.

The bad news is that once the "pavement" does return, it is often so poor that 10 mph seems very fast. The following 6 miles continue to roll wildly up and down through increasingly sere desert rangelands; aside from the road, the occasional cow is the only reminder that humans have passed by here before you.

Fourteen miles beyond Oheo Gulch the road ascends from near sea level through a seemingly interminable series of stair-step climbs to 1,900 feet where smooth highway pavement begins again near the Ulupalakua Ranch. Green trees and pastures also swoop down from above to greet you at this welcome outpost with its general store and nearby winery. Allow a minimum of 5 hours for this first 27 miles.

Many maps show a road down to Makena town on the beach. It is closed. Instead you continue on through idyllic green pastures populated by the occasional happy horse or cow. Though the road climbs another 1200 feet on the way to Keokea, the pavement and the grades are so much better than the earlier portion, you won't mind them at all. The views of central and west Maui get better and better. Allow 1 hour.

Keokea town is a joy to behold with 2 small stores, an art gallery, and Grandma's Coffee House stocked with all sorts of great fresh foods. The Highway becomes even more expertly graded and a wide shoulder is added.

Three miles beyond Keokea you pass the intersection with Highway 377 leading up the hill to the Haleakala. Shortly beyond the junction with Highway 377 you reach the summit of this ride at just over 3,000 feet. Kahului is 16 pedal-free miles down the hill. Though the shoulder is narrow for the next 6 miles, few cars will pass you as you fly down this lovely road. Kahului is about 1 hour away.

Forty-two miles from Oheo, Highway 37 passes the lower junction with Highway 37 and becomes a wide, well-paved 4-lane highway. Kahului is another 10 miles beyond and below. Enjoy the hard earned glide into town, and be cautious of strong crosswinds!

If you've not yet visited wonderful Makawao, this is a good time. Still on Highway 37, 0.3 miles beyond the junction with Highway 377 is the intersection with Highway 400. Makawao lays 2 miles away at the same elevation. For a description of Makawao, see the Kahului-Haleakala Route.

If you are riding the other direction from Makawao to Keokea, follow this route in reverse beginning at 9.5 miles through 24.4 miles from Kahului

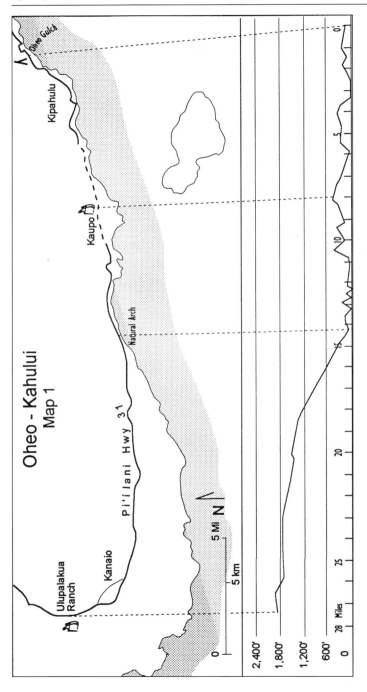

Oheo - Kahului
Map 1

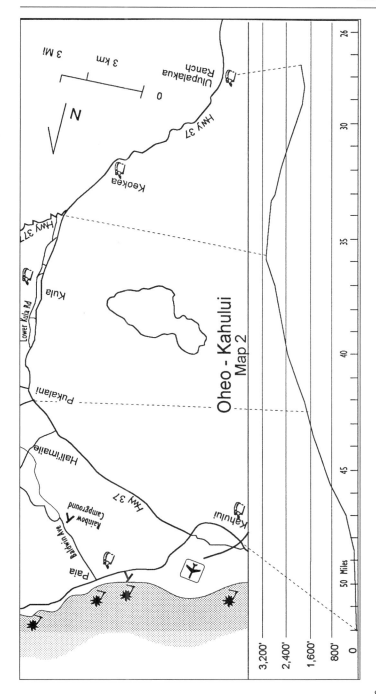

Oheo - Kahului
Map 2

all the way to the Tedeschi Winery. Touring this upland area, though strenuous, is delightful. The road from Keokea is a downhill rollick through green pastures and purple flowers on a beautifully paved and little used Highway.

Miles from Oheo	*Miles from Kahului*
0.0	*52.0*

Begin southeast (left as you face inland) on the highway at the entrance to the parking lot above the Haleakala Park Headquarters.

0.2
51.8
Leave Haleakala National Park.

0.9
51.1
Milepost 41. Enter Kipahulu town with numerous fruit and juice stands, but no store. Kipahulu is the turn-around point for motorist doing the day trip from points west; traffic, therefore, decreases considerably after leaving town.

1.0
51.0
Palapala Church. The grave of Charles Lindbergh rests in the nearby cemetery.

1.2
50.8
An especially pretty little gulch with hanging pools stair-stepping down to the sea.

2.3
49.7
Begin a steep 0.2 mile descent to sea level.

3.3
48.7
Cross a bridge and a sign identifying this as the Piilani Highway. Begin a very steep 0.3 mile long ascent.

3.9
48.1
Summit of this hill at 310 feet. The pavement ends here and a 4.5 mile long stretch of gravel-cobble-dirt-washboard road begins. The series of steep climbs and descents continues.

4.8
47.2
Back near sea level.

5.3
46.7
Top this hill at 220- foot elevation.

5.9
46.1
Bottom out at 90 feet.

6.2
45.8
Hui Aloha Church sited most scenically above Mokulao Landing since 1859. Note the church's the proximity to then Popoiwi Heiau a few hundred yards up the coast.

6.7
45.3
Milepost 35.

7.1
44.9
Kaupo General Store. The last store for 20.1 miles (hours are temperamental at best).

7.3
44.7
Auntie Jane's Fine Food, a lunch van in a pleasant field, presents plate lunches and the last cool drinks until the Mauka Snack Van 12.8 long, hot miles ahead. Jane doesn't get up early either.

7.4
44.6
The road rolls over several short hills for the next mile where the pavement begins again.

8.2
43.8
St. Joseph's Church, 1862. The summit of the Haleakala can be seen from the flower filled little churchyard. The verdant Kaupo Gap spills rain-bearing air out of the caldera directly above you. The dark green rain forest stands in marked contrast to the arid slope further to the west.

8.4
43.6
The blacktop begins anew. The hills continue to roll, but they get bigger.

8.7
43.3
Milepost 33.

9.2
42.8
Watch out for this very aggressive cattle guard at the bottom of the hill.

10.3
41.7
Begin a very steep 0.4-mile descent to sea level punctuated by yet another nasty cattle guard at the bottom.

12.0
40.0
Top of a small hill with especially good views both ahead and behind as the road twists through this very dry landscape. Enjoy the steep little glide into Wailaulau Gulch. It's not hard to imagine what this wide, boulder-strewn wash must look like in an angry flood.

12.2
39.8
Over the next 0.5 mile, drop and climb steeply through two successive gullies.
12.8
39.2
Milepost 29.

13.1
38.9
As you negotiate this downhill over deteriorating asphalt, look up long enough to spot a large natural arch in the sea cliffs ahead.

13.2
38.8
Begin another nasty little 150-foot climb followed by an exciting drop into the last seaside gully of this leg.

14.2
37.8
From this point just above sea level, the next 6 miles of road climbs gracelessly to an elevation of 1,520 feet.

14.4
37.6

The King's Highway foot path to La Perouse Bay begins here. I spoke to a ranch hand who claims to have seen mountain bikers traversing the lava-paved trail. From what I've seen of both ends of this "Highway," the paved road seems not so badly paved after all.

16.0
36.0

Milepost 26. You're at 600-foot elevation now.

17.9
34.1

Pass someone's lonely three-sided Homestead dwelling at 1,260-foot elevation.

18.5
33.5

You've climbed to 1,400 feet in elevation as you pass an old, extensive, piled-stone fence that extends to either side of the road. The grade eases for the next 7.4 miles.

19.9
32.1

Milepost 22.

20.0
32.0

As you top this hill you are rewarded with a view of red-topped Kahoolawe island. A little further on and you can see the Piilani Highway as it wends its way through dry scrublands far ahead of you. The road grade eases and surface improves for the next 3.8 miles.

22.9
29.1

Milepost 19.

23.8
28.2

The road surface gets bad again.

23.9
28.1

Milepost 23.9. At 1,766 feet you are entering the Homestead Community of Kanaio. Seaward, the peak of Pimoe cinder cone is at the same elevation as the road.

25.1
26.9
Mauka Snack Van . . . COLD DRINKS. Snack food is also served by these friendly folk.

25.6
26.4
Far below, the iridescent blue waters of La Perouse Bay glisten between two of the most recent lava flows on Maui. Beyond is tiny Molokini island. Note how the "green line" on the hills above dips ever lower as moisture-bearing winds invade this arid land. Soon you're riding through fragrant eucalyptus groves.

25.9
26.1
Start up a gnarly 0.7 mile, 300-foot climb.

26.6
25.4
Junction with Kanaio access road to the right here. Stay left and roll towards Ulupalakua Ranch. You've climbed to 1,975 feet!

27.1
24.9
Road surface improves . . . finally.
27.4
24.4
Tedeschi Winery. Heavily touristed, yet pretty little winery. They offer sampling, just remember that you're not at the top of the hill yet.

27.5
24.5
Ulupalakua Ranch Headquarters and General Store. This is a great place to replenish fluids and calories. Relax and give one of the rocking chairs on the front porch a little work out. The weather in this old west setting is usually cool and often cloudy, but seldom rainy. The next services are 5.4 miles ahead at Keokea.

After leaving Ulupalakua, drop down through mixed eucalyptus and green pasture for 1.0 mile.

28.5
23.5
At 1,805-foot elevation begin a 4.4-mile rolling climb up to Keokea town. If you've come all the way from Kipahulu this pavement and road will seem like a blessing. If you're just on a day ride from Kula or Makawao, this 1,050-foot climb may make you think less holy thoughts about the road.

In any case, do take time to marvel at the brilliant morning glories bordering the manicured green pastures as well as the excellent views of Makena, Wailea, and Kihei towns below you, and the mountains of west Maui across Ma'alaea Bay.

31.2
20.8
At the intersection with Kealakapu Road (a dead end) is a great viewpoint and a strange little park.

No restrooms or water, but really cool stone doggies. Sunny Kihei is directly below and looks best from this distance, in my opinion. You're at 2,350 feet here.

32.5
19.5
A small radio transmission tower in the forest to the right signals your approach to wonderful Keokea.

32.9
19.1
Intersection with the road to Kula Sanitarium. Welcome to Keokea with two stores, a gallery, and Grandma's Coffee House featuring fresh baked goodies, fresh food, and, yes, fresh coffee. It's an oasis. Grandma's is open 6:30 A.M. to 5:00 P.M. Monday through Saturday, 6:30 A.M. to 2:00 P.M. on Sundays. Fill a water bottle while you're here.

33.1
18.9
Keokea Park. Gnarly restrooms and equally gnarly tasting, but safe, water.

33.3
18.7
The highway grows shoulders here and varies from level to extremely well-graded up-hills for the next 2.5 miles.

33.7
18.3
Milepost 16.

35.3
16.7
3,000-foot elevation.

35.7
16.3
Junction with Highway 377 to Haleakala National Park. Turn right here to begin the 10,000-foot ascent of Haleakala. Highway 377 climbs steeply for

2.1 miles up to 3,700 feet before dropping down 1.0 mile to 3430 feet, where it intersects with Highway 378 (the road to the summit of the Haleakala). A description of the ride from that point can be found in the Kahului-Haleakala Route. This route guide to Kahului continues straight here.

Highway 31 becomes Highway 37 at this junction.

35.8
16.2
At 3,085 feet this is the summit of the Oheo-Kahului route. It's all downhill from here, bruddahs an' sistas!

It's 6.4 miles to the intersection with Highway 377. Unfortunately, the shoulder disappears again. Traffic, however, is generally light and your speed is generally pretty fast on this long descent. YAHOO!

35.9
16.1
Rice Memorial Park offers the usual challenging restrooms, but also offers good water and picnicking with a nice view.

36.6
15.4
Point of Interest: The road to the right (uphill) quickly turns onto Lower Kula Road which leads you down through tiny one-store Kula town and the distinctively octagonal and very white Holy Ghost Church. This landmark is visible from all of central Maui as well as the summit of the Haleakala.

Alternate: If the narrow lanes of the Highway bother you, Lower Kula Road can be used as an alternate route down through Kula and continues, with one break, for 5 miles.

37.8
14.2
The road to the right takes you uphill to Kula town and the Holy Ghost Church. You're at 2,600 feet here.

40.7
11.3
Lower junction with Lower Kula Road. If climbing up this grade towards Keokea, a left turn here will take you up the hill on a much less busy, and less well-paved and graded road. Rejoin the shoulderless Highway 377 in about 5 miles, 0.7 miles short of the upper junction with Highway 377.

42.2
9.8
Lower junction with Highway 377 up to the Haleakala. You're at 1,730-foot elevation. Generous shoulders return. Continue straight to Kahului.

42.5
9.5

Continue straight to Kahului. The junction with Highway 400 to Makawao and Paia or Hana for the ambitious. Charming Makawao is 1.6 miles to the right for a relaxing upcountry detour (see the Kahului-Haleakala route for a description).

Highway 37 rolls downhill for the next 7.8 miles. As you drop through the next 1,700 vertical feet from the cool, cloudy upland you're likely to experience a temperature increase of 5-15 degrees. Certainly one thing you'll want to avoid experiencing is crashing your bike here so close to the Airport and in front of such a large audience. To avoid such embarrassment, be aware, as you gaze across at the West Maui mountains and the Iao Valley above Wailuku, that the shoulder has been strewn with clods of slick and adhesive mud from the tires of cane and pineapple trucks as they've entered the road. Also be aware of seemingly hurricane-force crosswinds ripping through the pineapple fields from the east.

50.0
2.0

Junction with Highway 36. Turn left here to Kahului. A right turn leads towards Hana, straight ahead to the Kahului Airport.

Mile 33.6 of the Kahului-Haleakala route. A group of pink jump-suited "cruisers" glide down the treeless upper portion of Highway 378 at 8,000 feet above sea level.

50.5
1.5
Exit to Pu'unene and Kihei on the left side of the Highway.
52.0
0.0
Junction with Highway 380-Dairy Road in Kahului. You're back to the beginning of the Kahului-Hana route.

Mile nine on the Oheo-Kahului route. The patchy black topped road of Highway 31 stretches ahead into the desert of Southern Maui, which lies in the rain shadow of the Haleakala rising 10,000 feet into the clouds.

Chapter 3

Moloka'i

Moloka'i is the oldest of the three Maui County islands. The west Moloka'i shield began building 1.5 million years ago. The final major volcanic episodes on the more massive east shield occurred 1.2 million years ago, leaving a large caldera slightly higher than 5,000 feet.

The high mountains in the east wring up to 160" of rain from the sky each year, yet just 5 miles away average rainfall decreases to 20 inches annually. These high mountains meet the trade winds first, leaving the rest of the island in its rain shadow. As you travel from east to west the vegetation goes from lush tropical forest, to scrubby grasslands, and finally to savannah-like near desert. If it's raining where you are, west Moloka'i is likely dry.

Moloka'i hasn't always been so dry. Prior to the *haole* conquest, Moloka'i supported between 8,000 and 40,000 people. The 70 coastal fishponds provided a rich aquaculture and there is considerable evidence of rotating burn and plow agriculture far up the hillsides. Introduction of grazing stock, initially to feed the crews of visiting ships, led to such severe over-grazing and consequent erosion that most of the fishponds are now filled with mud and the cloudline on the mountains has actually been raised 1,000 feet upslope.

The nurturing Halawa Valley is one of the oldest continually inhabited sites in all of Hawaii: its first settlers arrived around 650 A.D. Although Moloka'ians developed a thriving economy over the next 800 years, they were constantly being invaded by their larger neighbors from Oahu and Maui. Beginning around 1500 A.D., the ruling ali'i began to foster a new and powerful shamanistic cult of Kahuna. Their *mana*, or spiritual power, grew so strong that it was an accepted fact throughout the islands that the Kahuna could chant their enemies to death. When Captain Cook arrived in 1788, Moloka'i was known as the forbidden island.

If you visit Moloka'i today, you may notice that the tourist bureau has titled it "the friendly island." The plethora of locked gates, "keep out" signs, and camouflage painted trucks may make you feel less than welcome. The fact is that Moloka'i has become one of the focal points of the current native revolt against *haole* rule. Early in this century various land reform acts set aside most of the portion of Moloka'i not already bought up by *haoles* for native lands. Subsequently most of this land was also accumulated into *haole* ownership via various schemes and skullduggery.

The situation now is such that Hawaiians control much of the eastern portion of Moloka'i not included in the Highland Forest Preserve. Here

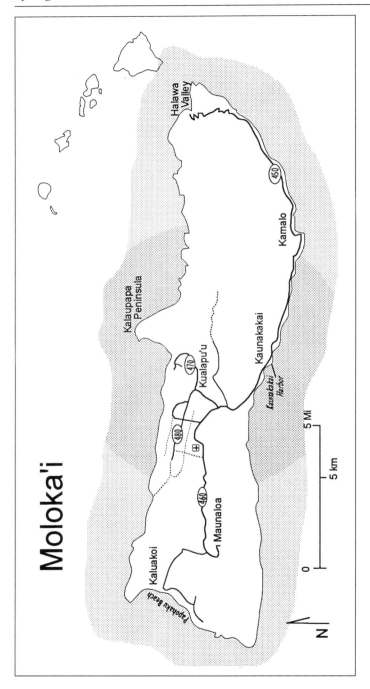

many are trying to work their *kuleana* farms in traditional ways, and *haole* tourists are not part of their vision of paradise. You might notice cars with illegal "Sovereign Nation" license plates in place of Hawaiian plates.

The portion of the island west of Kaunakakai is largely owned by Moloka'i Ranch, a subsidiary of the Castle and Cook Corporation. Their attitude seems to be to maximize profits, and unless you want to give them some money, you also are not part of their corporate vision of the future.

The result of this juxtaposition makes Moloka'i somewhat less than a "friendly island." The good news is that due to the low flow of tourists, Moloka'i retains a sleepy, small town feeling; and though the residents are seldom effusive in their greetings of strangers, they are at least respectful and grudgingly tolerant. Like anywhere else in the world, your smile is usually returned with a smile.

Getting There

As is the case with Lana'i, there are two ways to get to Moloka'i: you can either fly or take the ferry. Unlike Lana'i, air service is a bit more frequent and flexible and a trip through the Honolulu Airport isn't always necessary if flying interisland from Hawaii or Kauai. Remember that island hoppers do charge approximately $50 each time you check a bike on board. Check with the airlines listed in the "Getting There" chapter, or with your travel agent, for availability. There are no direct flights to Moloka'i from the mainland.

If you are already on Maui, the Maui Princess Ferry (1-800-533-5800) makes the 90-minute round trip from Kaunakakai to Lahaina, Maui twice each day. Best of all, the fare is only $25 each way, there is no charge for bicycles, and the morning trip back to Kaunakakai includes a free fruit and muffin breakfast. The Princess sails from Kaunakakai at 5:30 A.M. and 3:55 P.M. and returns from Lahaina at 7:00 A.M. and 5:00 P.M.. Because the ship is too large to dock at Lahaina harbor, a smaller charter boat takes you from slip #3 (not from the public boat landing) out to the ferry and then brings arriving passengers back to shore. The result is that the ship leaves Lahaina before it arrives.

Names and Numbers

Write the Moloka'i Chamber of Commerce at P.O. Box 515, Kaunakakai, HI 96748. Or call the Visitors Association at 1-800-800-6367 for a free brochure.

Camping

Due to the current anal temperament regarding land ownership, unofficial camping may be a little more adventuresome than on Maui or Lana'i. Fortunately there are many fine official campgrounds on Moloka'i:

Maui County Parks at Moloka'i Division of Parks, P.O. Box 1055, Kaunakakai, Hawaii 96748 (808) 553-3204. $3 nightly fee for permit and reservation, both available by mail.

One (pronounced *oh-ne*) Ali'i County Park is just three miles east of Kaunakakai. It offers beach-side camping in a small palm grove (beware of falling coconuts) near one of the many fishponds along the coast. The Park has toilets, drinking water, open air enclosed showers, and covered picnic areas. Due to its proximity to town, it also offers visits by reggae-blasting pick-up trucks, and heavy use by townsfolk. The place quiets down by 10:00 P.M.

Papohaku Beach County Park sits jewel-like upon the two-mile-long Popohaku Beach at Moloka'is' wild west end. Except for the ubiquitous Hawaiian family that always seems to be living there, Papohaku is marvelously yours. It offers enclosed showers, excellent water (imported from the northeastern rain forest), clean restrooms, and cool shady grass to camp on. This is a destination in itself.

Halawa County Park nestles at the mouth of the verdant Halawa Valley at the northeast end of Moloka'i. The park itself doesn't offer camping, however, free camping is available on the grassy shore a short walk away. The park has a partially enclosed shower. There are also restrooms, and water for which treatment with iodine or chlorine is recommended.

Pala'au State Park, Division of State Parks, P.O. Box 1049, Wailuku-Maui, Hawaii 96793. Camping permits are free. This often-rainy campground is near the Kalaupapa Overlook in a wonderful tropical forest. There are restrooms provided but the water requires purification.

Kiowea Park, 2 miles west of Kaunakakai, neighbors a large historic palm grove hugging a low stretch of coastline. Kiowea Park offers showers and perhaps a little more evening quiet, however, the highway is busier here than at One Ali'i Park 5 miles east. Kiowea is primarily an organizational park administered by the Department of Hawaiian Homelands. If you are booking less than 1 year ahead of your trip, don't bother to call the overworked secretary at (808) 567-6104. The fee for camping is $5 per night.

Other Accommodations

Most of the available rooms are concentrated at the west end of the island at Kaluakoi (808) 552-2555 and start at $100. Less expensive rooms are available near Kaunakakai at:

Hotel Moloka'i, (800) 423-6656: Doubles from $60.

Pau Hana Inn, (800) 423-6656: Doubles from $50.

Groceries

Although there are small markets in Maunaloa and at Kaluakoi at the west end, Kaunakakai is *da kine* place to have *da* groceries. There are two supermarkets (both closed Sunday afternoon) and a small natural food store (open Sunday afternoon but closed on Saturday). The Kanemitsu Bakery opens at 5:30 A.M. to serve breakfasts and lunches as well as some really fine grain and fruit breads, closed on Tuesday. All of these are on a two-block stretch of Ala Malama Street in downtown Kaunakakai.

Restaurants

Kaunakakai offers the Moloka'i Drive-In, a new Pizza Cafe, and the Holo Holo Kai at the Hotel Moloka'i 2 miles east of town for more upscale cuisine. Maunaloa has JoJo's, open for lunch and dinner only. Finally, on the way up to Pala'au State Park, the Kualapu'u Cook House in Kualapu'u on Farrington Avenue offers hearty meals to celebrate you on your way ($3.50 for a big, sloppy burger), closed Sunday.

Other Services

Most of the services offered on Moloka'i are offered on or near the three central blocks of Ala Malama Street in Kaunakakai which includes a pharmacy, the post office, a medical clinic, a bank machine, a water sports store, and the police station (911 works on Moloka'i). The Laundromat is behind the natural food store.

If you arrive by boat, downtown Kaunakakai is nearby. From the Kaunakakai Landing take Kaunakakai Road inland for 0.7 miles. The large intersection there marks the beginning of Maunaloa Highway 460 to the west (left), the Kamehameha V Highway 450 to the east (right), and Ala Malama Road through downtown Kaunakakai is straight ahead. This intersection is also the starting point for the routes to Halawa and Papohaku.

Kaunakakai—Halawa Valley

This 27.5-mile route follows the coastline for the first 21 miles. It remains virtually free of hills until it begins to climb over a 700-foot high pasture and forest-draped shoulder. After passing by the Pu'u o Hoku Ranch the road drops sharply down to beautifully isolated Halawa Valley with its waterfalls, tropical forest, and beach-side camping area. Allow at least 3 hours without side trips for this ride.

The flat portion of the route rolls past views of several of the ancient aquaculture fishponds constructed over the past 1,300 years. The protective reef along the south coast is up to one mile wide, so coastal waters are generally shallow. Unfortunately, extensive overgrazing by imported cattle on the hillsides above has resulted in the silting in of several of these once valuable ponds. Imported mangroves have further obscured the now-muddy portions of this coast.

If the trade winds are up when you intend to ride this section of coast, you can mitigate their effects by starting early in the day before they get strong. Fortunately most of this trip is embedded in low tropical forests which help to break the force of the winds. The good news is that the winds can also blow you effortlessly back to Kaunakakai on your return trip.

The South coast of Moloka'i tends to be warm, sunny, and sparsely populated. Beyond One Ali'i Park, Wavecrest Resort offers the only water source until Halawa Park, so bring a little extra beverage with you and fill your water bottles at One Ali'i Park just east of Kaunakakai.

95

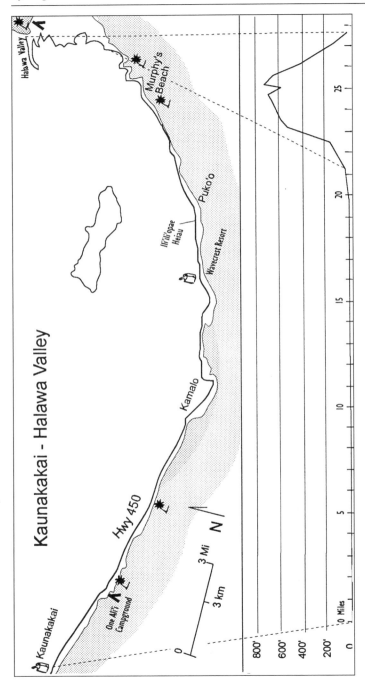

Kaunakakai - Halawa Valley

The importance of spirituality in the lives of native Moloka'ians is evidenced by numerous *Heiaus* along this coast. Several can be seen and at least one easily visited.

The further away from Kaunakakai you get, the narrower the road becomes. Fortunately, the traffic decreases proportionately. The last 6 miles of the ride is newly paved and it is a joy to ride along this little-used single-lane country road.

The gem of this trip waits for you at the end of the road in tiny Halawa Valley where the County Park offers an outdoor shower and fresh water which should be treated before drinking. After dropping over three waterfalls, the Halawa River winds through a homesteaded plain to a small harboring bay. The trails up to the falls cross several homesteaded *kuleanas* upon which you are generally not welcome. If you wish to hike the greasy, boulder-strewn paths, ask around in Kaunakakai. You'll meet the holder of permission within 4 or 5 inquiries.

Camping in the midst of this splendor is free.

Miles from Kaunakakai	Miles from Halawa Valley
0.0	*27.6*

Junction of Kaunakakai Road to the ferry boat dock with Ala Malama Avenue to central Kaunakakai. The Maunaloa Highway 460 heads west to Maunaloa and Papohaku Beach. Turn onto Kamehameha V Highway 450 to the east.

2.0
25.6
Milepost 2. The glass-strewn shoulder ends but so does local traffic.

2.9
24.7
Point of Interest: The *makai* turn-off gives you a good view of 1 of over 40 ancient fishponds along this coast.

3.2
24.4
One Ali'i Park. Good water, enclosed but cool showers, and camping. Lanai stretches out across the narrow channel to your right. West Maui is also visible down the coast to the east. This is the last drinking water available until Halawa Park.

5.6
22.0
Kakahaia Park. Picnic facilities.

9.8
17.8
Enter the loosely bound settlement of Kamalo. No services.

10.6
17.0
Pretty little 1870s St. Joseph Church and cemetery.

10.7
16.9
Watch for a sign to the right to "Smith-Bronte Landing." In 1927 at this site, two pilots crash landed when they ran out of gas en route to Honolulu thus "successfully" completing the first commercial flight from the mainland to the Hawaiian islands.

12.9
14.7
Wavecrest Resort and grocery store. This is a welcome and wet oasis on this often very hot and dry ride. Local bananas are $.25 each.

While you're cooling off at the resort, notice that the forest boundary "green line" on the mountains above you is descending as you travel east toward the origin of the moisture-bearing trade winds.

13.3
14.3
On the hillside just beyond the Wavecrest Resort are six *heiaus*, several visible from the Kilohana school yard. This was obviously a seat of power in the pre-colonial times.

14.6
13.0
Our Lady of the Sorrows Church (1874) is opposite the large Niaupala Fishpond.

15.3
12.3
Hawaii's largest mango patch also offers horse cart rides and demonstrations of Hawaiian crafts. Sound like a tourist trap? It's not. These humble people are sincere in their desire to share this small portion of their heritage with you. Check it out.

15.4
12.2
0.15 miles past the entrance to the mango patch is a road to one of the largest *heiaus* in the area and is well worth the visit, but it isn't easy to find.

A few feet beyond fire hydrant #45 is a short bridge. Immediately after the bridge a gravel road leads inland. The Ili'ili'opae Heiau is 0.35 miles up this road which parallels a normally dry stream bed as it enters a moist and shady forest. As you reach a private house look to the left for a sign disavowing liability should the hiker continue on this 12-hour-minimum trek. The *heiau* is 100 meters up the trail. This beautiful multitiered platform was built from stones imported via human chains from the west end of the island. Hawaii wasn't always paradisical for the early Hawaiians. This trail continues up over the pali at about 5,000-feet elevation.

20.5
7.1
Murphey's Beach County Park begins across the road from the Moanui Sugar Mill ruins. No restrooms or water, fine beach and snorkeling in incredibly clear, reef, protected water. This is a fine place to stop and enjoy lunch and marvel at the closeness of west Maui across the Pailolo Channel. This is the last long strand of sand accessible on the south coast.

The Highway becomes a newly paved one-lane road at this point.

20.2
6.8
The coast line for the next 1.3 miles becomes rocky. This is Monk seal habitat in the winter. Look for them but do not approach them. Contact with you could mean death for them.

21.3
6.3
Start da climb at 45-foot elevation.

22.0
5.6
Slowly leave the coast as the Highway rolls over tree-speckled pasture.

22.4
5.2
A right hairpin turn in a deep gully at 165-foot elevation. Watch for frequent wet and slick road conditions in this upland area.

23.3
4.3
A right hairpin at the bottom of a deep gulley. Elevation 525 feet. The grade eases considerably here as the road rounds a seaward bluff at 600 feet and enters a grassy plateau reminiscent of the English countryside.

25.0
2.6
At Milepost 25 pass the headquarters of Puu O Hoku Ranch which advertises vacation rentals. Elevation here is 680 feet. Immediately after the Ranch, drop 100 feet in 0.1 miles then climb back up to 710 feet over the next 0.2 miles.

25.8
1.8
From 655 feet begin a breathtaking descent into Halawa Valley.

26.1
1.5
In 0.35 miles drop 230 feet. This sharp corner features a wide shoulder viewpoint of the beach at Halawa Bay 425 feet below. Three of the Halawa Valley waterfalls can be seen in the canyon towards the high mountains.

27.1
0.6
A beautiful 1.0-mile-long traverse down the mountainside brings you to this hairpin turn at 130-foot elevation.

27.6
0.0
Pass Halawa Beach County Park. Restrooms, cool outdoor shower, and drinking water that requires purification are available here.

The pavement ends a few feet further on and a small community of temporary homes occupied by tolerant natives lines the path to the grassy platform next to the sea. Several primitive campsites are available. Swimming is especially good at the crescent beach nestled below the cliff you just rode down.

There is no loop return available back to Kaunakakai so simply retrace this marvelous road.

Pala'au State Park—Mo'omomi Bay

This route takes you up a very vigorous climb from the dry lowlands of central Moloka'i up to the often-rainwashed Pala'au State Park 5.8 miles from Kaunakakai. Within the Park are breathtaking views of the central Moloka'i isthmus and, from the edge of a 1,600-foot cliff, a view of the Kalaupapa Peninsula, now a National Historic Park. This geologically young Kalaupapa Peninsula was extruded long after the tremendous erosion of these highest of the world's seacliffs. This abject isolate served as an exile for Hawaiians afflicted with Hansen's Disease, or leprosy, caused by a bacterium found in the fresh waters of Hawaii.

The park is also the sight of the much-post-carded Phallic Rock, mule rides, and guided hikes down to the Kalaupapa Peninsula, and a

State Campground. The Pala'au campground consists of several primitive and often soggy sites clustered around a deeply graveled parking lot, all in a beautiful tropical forest of cypress, ironwood, and *koa* trees. The restrooms are old but serviceable. There are no showers here. There is water but campers are warned to treat water with iodine or chlorine before drinking.

Before beginning this ride a quick look at the local weather may save you some disappointment. Typically, the weather over Pala'au State Park is controlled by moist trade winds blowing from the east. As this warm air is lifted by the mass of the 5,000-foot high eastern Moloka'i mountains, the air cools and clouds condense. The result is often a narrow cloud plume stretching downwind, often all the way to Papohaku at the west end. As a consequence the land below this cloud plume is often shrouded in fog or rain. I once left the Pala'au campground in a cold, soaking rain and stopped to dry out with a sunny, warm picnic in Kualapu'u less than 4 miles away.

If the weather looks bad above you, consider visiting Pala'au on your way back from Papohaku if you're going to the west end. To approach from the west, turn left on Highway 480 just over 1.0 mile east of the Moloka'i Airport. Follow 480 1.4 miles to the intersection with Farrington Avenue where you turn right up the hill to Kualapu'u.

If starting from Kaunakakai, follow the Kaunakakai-Papohaku Route on Highway 460 West 4.1 miles to the junction with Highway 470 where this route begins.

Allow 1.5 hours to reach Pala'au Park and an additional 2.5 to 3 hours for the Mo'omomi Bay portion from Kaunakakai.

From Junct. Highway 460/470 0.0	*From Junct. Highway* *460/Hauakea Ave.* *23.1*

Intersection of Highways 460 and 470. This route begins at 470 feet and climbs to 1660 feet in 4.8 miles. Begin your ride north up the steeper Highway 470.

1.1
22.0
The long straight stretch of road ends with a gentle right curve at 770 feet. The grade eases a little for 1.0 mile before increasing again.

1.7
21.4
Kualapu'u town. Limited services. Intersection with Highway 480 and Farrington Avenue which leads down to Mo'omomi Bay. Continue up the hill to Pala'au.

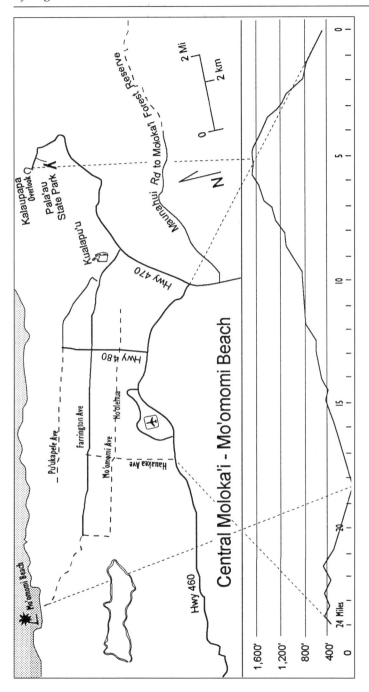

Central Moloka'i - Mo'omomi Beach

2.4
20.7
Pass a radio installation to the left as you climb steeply through the forested valley.

3.4
19.7
A well-paved road leads to the right. You're at 1,395-foot elevation as you climb through thickening forest broken by green pastures. You're entering the rain belt created by the cloud plume formed by the east Moloka'i mountains. Stay straight on Highway 470.

4.3
18.5
The highway improves noticably and shoulders widen as you approach the Pala'au State Park boundary.

4.7
18.1
Summit at 1675 feet. The newly paved road rolls gently along the ridge for 1.0 more mile.

5.6
17.5
The campground is to the left here at the sign.

5.8
17.3
The road ends here at a parking lot. To the right is a short trail leading to the Lookout. A dizzying 1,600 feet below you stretches Kalaupapa Peninsula, formerly an isolated leper colony, and now a National Historic Park. To visit, you must go with a guided trip. Check with the headquarters 0.1 miles before the campground for further information.

A slightly longer trail (0.3 miles) leads through a wet conifer forest to Kaule o Nanahoa, also known as Phallic Rock. With a little help from human hands, this boulder has come to vaguely resemble an erect penis (what doesn't?). It is said that any woman sleeping under the rock for a night will be blessed with child. Be careful where you sleep around here.

Again, there is no loop available to the cyclist without a full set of Ranch keys to open the many locked gates so head back down Highway 470 retracing your track 4.1 miles to the intersection with Highway 480 and Farrington Avenue in Kualapu'u town.

9.9
13.2
Kualapu'u town and the intersection with Highway 480. Turn right here to proceed towards Ho'olehua Homesteads and Mo'omomi Beach.

10.1
13.0
Glide past central Ho'olehua with a sometimes-open grocery and the Kualapu'u Cook House (closed Sundays) on your right. Roll past Moloka'i High School.

11.8
11.3
Begin a 2.5-mile glide downhill, pedal-free run. The central Moloka'i isthmus streches out before you. Most of this arid land was set aside for Native Homeland development and so still maintains a healthy low-forest cover rather than the now-bankrupt, earth scarring, erosion-prone, pineapple operation.

12.3
10.8
Intersection with Highway 480. Turn *makai* off Highway 470 to get to Mo'omomi Beach. Highway 480 is the last paved road south to Highway 460 and the west end of Moloka'i. The Moloka'i Airport is 3 miles *mauka* here. The route rolls on over gentle hills.

14.6
8.5
4.7 miles from the intersection back in Ho'olehua as the Highway begins a noticeable dip, Hauakea Avenue, a good wide red-earth road leaves Farrington Avenue to the left climbing a slight hill to Highway 460. You will come back to Hauakea Avenue later on this route if your eventual destination is western Moloka'i.

15.0
8.1
Top of a small hill with a commanding view of the lowlands stretching towards the coast and Mo'omomi Bay. This is a good turn-around point for the less determined. Bear in mind that strong tail winds now will be in your face on the way back up this hill.

15.4
7.7
The pavement ends and the surface becomes well-packed earth. If dry, this is a very ridable surface. Be cautious of deep dust accumulations that can cause your wheels to go in unexpected directions.
The road continues for 2.5 miles as it drops 310 feet in elevation.

17.9
5.2

Mo'omomi Bay. This wind swept beach has been so little used over the years that it has survived as habitat for several indigenous species. To help preserve this unique area the Nature Conservancy has agreed to steward this scenic wild shore. An extensive sand dune belt begins at the far end of this beach and flows uphill driven by nearly constant trade winds.

Again, without keys to the many, many locked gates, the offroad cyclist is denied several potential loop routes and must instead return from whence you came; backtrack 3.3 miles up Farrington Avenue.

21.2
1.9

Back up to red dirt Hauakea Avenue. Turn right up this pineapple haul road. Climb a little hill then drop down to Mo'omomi Avenue.

21.8
1.3

Cross Mo'omomi Avenue. If the Trades are blowing for you, you'll hardly need to pedal up these small rises.

22.3
0.8

Cross Keonelele Avenue. Stay straight.

23.1
0.0

Hauakea Avenue ends at the intersection with Highway 460. You are now at Mile 8.5 from Kaunakakai on the Kaunakakai-Papohaku Route. You may now follow the Kaunakakai-Papohaku Route back to Kaunakakai to the left, or continue on to Papohaku Beach or Maunaloa town to the right. Both options are described in the following section.

Kaunakakai—Papohaku Beach

Papohaku Beach County Park is sited near the northeast end of the longest beach in all of Hawaii. The campground itself is pleasant enough to warrant a visit. The tent areas are grassy and wonderfully shaded. The indoor showers are attached to clean restrooms and the water is eminently drinkable, though its importation from the east has been a bone of contention with homesteading natives in the Hoolehua area. The view from the beach includes the island Oahu, faint in the haze across the Kaiwi Channel. At night, the lights of Honolulu glow eerily.

The area around the Park provides several options for day rides and exploration by foot. Because it lies in the rain shadow of the massive east Moloka'i mountains, the west end is dry and sunny. Gener-

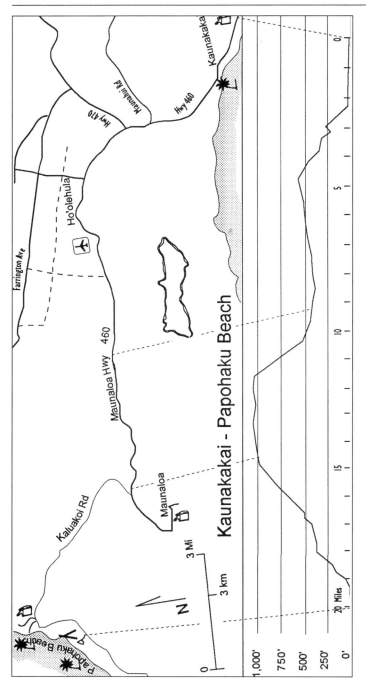

Kaunakakai - Papohaku Beach

ally, this isolated region is just about the perfect place for a relaxed, camping vacation.

Before leaving Kaunakakai consider that groceries are scarce and expensive on the west end of Moloka'i, available only at the small store in Maunaloa and at the commissary at Kaluakoi Resort. So stock up at one of the three markets here in town.

The route begins in semi-arid Kaunakakai and rises to an increasingly arid central isthmus via a 2.5-mile, 600-foot climb. From this point the trade winds begin to push you along through sporadically failing pineapple fields. The Highway can be seen snaking over the northern shoulder of the west Moloka'i mountains in the distance.

After passing the Moloka'i Airport, the highway makes a demanding 2.5-mile climb to the west Moloka'i highlands. The route then takes Kaluakoi Road back down to sea level past the Kaluakoi Resort and on to Papohaku Beach.

There is no reliable water source along this dry and sunny route, so take some extra with you. Allow 2 to 3 hours for this route.

Miles from Kaunakakai	*Miles from Papohaku Beach*
0.0	*20.1*

Junction of Highways 450 East and 460 West at Kaunakakai. Take Highway 460 West.

0.7
19.4
Milepost 1.

1.0
19.1
Keowea Park. An organizational park administered by the Hawaiian Homelands Association.

1.1
19.0
Kapuaiwa Coconut Grove. These 10 acres contain over 1,000 trees planted by Kamehameha V in the 1860s. Across the road is a charming row of churches, old and new.

2.2
17.9
Kalaniana'ole Homestead Colony on the right. To the left, below the Hawaiian Research Center a dirt road winds off along the coast for several miles toward Hale O Lono Harbor. Unfortunately, this good dirt track is eventually blocked by a locked gate at the boundary with the Moloka'i Ranch.

The road stretches straight ahead as it climbs to the junction with Highway 470 in three distinct pitches.

4.1
16.0
Junction with Highway 470 at 470 feet. Continue straight on Highway 460. A great view has opened up behind you. The mangrove-lined south coast of Moloka'i stretches in both directions with Lana'i floating above the Kalohi Channel.

Highway 470, to the right here, offers an alternate route which takes you to the Kalaupapa Overlook and is detailed in the Kaunakakai-Mo'omomi route log.

4.7
15.4
Milepost 5. This is the top of the grade out of Kaunakakai at 607 feet in elevation. Highway 460 is visible as it snakes up the west Moloka'i mountains ahead.

5.6
14.5
Occasional Homesteaders' craft and vegetable stands to the right.

5.8
14.3
Continue the gentle glide downhill pass the junction with Highway 480 which leads to Ho'olehua settlement (no services).

6.9
13.2
Roll over some small hills as you pass the Moloka'i Airport.

8.5
11.6
Connection of Mo'omoni Beach route. Junction with Hauakea Avenue, a red-earth road which leads to Mo'omomi Beach. The alternate route to Pala'au State Park rejoins this route at this point. Elevation here is 365 feet.

9.0
11.1
Begin to climb gently.

10.9
9.2
Just beyond a water tank on the right a dirt road crosses the

highway, elevation 785 feet. There is a fine view of the north side of
Moloka'i. Some long-lived sand dunes (over 20,000 years old) can be
seen stretching from their source above Mo'omomi Beach to the
northwest.

11.5
8.6
Top of the hill (more or less) at 1085 feet.

11.9
8.2
Top one of several rolling hills encountered over the next 2.5 miles.
Great views are unveiled around each turn in this high country. Notice
that each and every side road comes complete with a locked gate and a no
trespassing sign, courtesy of the Moloka'i Ranch.

14.6
5.5
Turn right onto Kaluakoi Road as it begins its 1,010-foot descent to Papohaku Beach Park.

Side trip

Maunaloa Town Side Trip:
1.8 miles further down the road, tiny Maunaloa makes an enjoyable side trip before heading down to Papohaku or a good day trip up from the Beach if you're camping for a few days. Originally begun as a homesteading center, through various land grab
schemes in the 1920s, the precursor to the Moloka'i ranch grabbed this end of the island and tried pineapple plantations with water imported from the wet northwestern
valleys. Maunaloa became a plantation town. Still in the clutches of the Moloka'i Ranch,
residents eke out livings in the shadow of the "Company."

0.0
Intersection of Highway 460 with Kaluakoi Road. Continue west on Highway
460. Roll over small hills as the west end of Moloka'i unfolds below you. In the distance
to the west you can see the island Oahu through the haze across the Kaiwi Channel. Diamond Head's distinctive profile rises from the sea at the extreme left of the island.

1.1
Maunaloa town greets you *mauka* (toward the summit) of the Highway as you
swing around a left curve in the road. The extent of the land used for cattle grazing becomes apparent on the slope below you.

1.5
Climb a small hill as you enter town.

Side trip cont.

1.7

The Moloka'i Ranch is headquartered in the large barn-like building on your right across from the gas station. Here you can pay $10 for the right to ride down to Hale O Lono Harbor. The road is open Friday evening through Sunday evening, or stop by and learn about not trespassing on Ranch lands.

1.8

Post Office and Central Business District, home to a few galleries and craft shops, a thinly stocked grocery store, and Jo Jo's restaurant (open Monday to Saturday; Lunch from 12:00–2:00 and Dinner from 5:00–7:45). You can get a fine picnic lunch and enjoy it alfresco on the general store's front porch or amble across the street and dine at the shaded tables in front of or behind the Post Office, where locals play card games.

2.0

Top of the town with a school, a community center, and an undeveloped park.

2.1

End of pavement in 1996. Return the same way you came in.

In 1995, The Moloka'i Ranch evicted nearly all of the residents from the old plantation style houses on the south side of town and bull-dozed down to bare earth. The plan is to build new expensive homes in a subdivision from Hell. I have no idea who will buy these homes. Most of the locals I spoke with said that employment was difficult to non-existent.

Back on the route:

14.6
5.5
Kaluakoi Road begins its 1,010-foot descent to Papohaku Beach Park 5.5 miles away.

17.7
2.4
Intersection with a well-paved road to the left. Stay straight here.

18.1
2.0
The final downhill pitch takes you down to the coastal plain in 1.1 miles.

19.1
1.0
Paved Kapuhi Road leads to the right here. The Kaluakoi Resort with its small store is 0.4 miles down Kapuhi Road. Continue on main road for Papohaku.

19.3
0.8
The road becomes level as it begins a run through a very African-looking acacia and tall grass forest. Note the "Wild Turkey Crossing" sign. They're not kidding.

20.1
0.0
Entrance to Papohaku Park to the right at the large sign. 0.1 miles ahead the Parks clean restrooms and indoor, yet brisk, showers await. Two rectangular camping areas are to your right. Read the signs regarding the lawn irrigation schedule to avoid unpleasant early morning surprises.

Side trip

Papohaku Side Trips
Southwest of the campground, Kaluakoi Road continues as a well-paved road for 3.5 miles, offering 5 additional beach access points. The route is described below.
0.0
Begin at the entrance to Papohaku Beach Park. Turn right onto Kaluakoi Road.

0.6
A right turn here leads you 0.2 miles to a parking lot (more than likely empty). The central portion of Papohaku lies beyond the acacia-studded foredune.

1.0
Climb a small hill for the next 0.3 miles. From its top you can see Maunaloa town above with its complement of tall Norfolk pines.

1.3
At the top of the hill Papapa Place drops steeply to the right and ends at a parking lot and access to the west end of Papohaku Beach. There is a shower and foot wash at the trail head here.

1.8
Turn right down the hill at this T-intersection.

2.2
Intersection with a subdivision road. A right turn here on Kulawai Road followed by a left at the first opportunity 0.3 miles downhill and another right after 0.1 miles brings you to a 0.1 mile access road which ends at a small cove nestled in an old volcanic cone. Cool. Showers and water available.

2.4
Poolau Beach access road. A sandy strip above a rocky beach. Showers and water available.

2.9

Kapaa Beach access. Some small sandy tidepools await 0.1 miles down this road. Showers available.

3.5

The end of the paved road is met with, what else? A locked gate.

The short beach access road here leads you to a small, private, nearly enclosed cove, protected from waves and currents, a perfect swimming spot. This small cove is made all the more perfect by its lining of sugary sand. Here too, is an outdoor shower and fresh water. Enjoy.

There is no loop available here, so simply return the way you came.

Northeast of the campground are some golf course-lined coves and the Kaluakoi Resort.

0.0

Turn left on Kaluakoi Road from the Park entrance.

1.0

Kapuhi Place is on the left here. The Resort Center is 0.4 miles down this road at its end.

The Kaluakoi Resort has telephones, restrooms, a small formal garden, a formal dining room, a really good snack bar open until 5:00 with garden-side alfresco dining, a general store open 9 A.M.—7 P.M. everyday, and a Liberty House Department store outlet. All of this on a charmingly small scale.

1.04

Turn left on Kakaako Road and follow it 0.4 miles through the golf course to Lio Place. Turn left on Lio Place. Continuing straight on Kakaako Road seems interesting but ends in a locked gate 0.7 miles on. Lio Place soon turns into a bad dirt road. Pursue it just 0.1 miles further. Walk your bike across the fairway of the golf course to a pretty little sand-lined cove. A foot trail here wends along the coast to reveal more clear water, rocky coves. Snorkeling is inviting here, however the currents are very powerful and the inexperienced should stay out of the water.

Again there is no loop available here so return the way you came.

Chapter 4

Lana'i

Lana'i is the least visited and least developed of all the major Hawaiian islands. Because it sits squarely in the rain shadow of the cloud wringing Haleakala on Maui, Lana'i is arid; its east side receives less than 10 inches of rain per year.

Pre-contact Hawaiians understood this well and used the island almost solely for fishing. Petroglyphs distinct from those found elsewhere in the islands indicate the evolution of a separate Lana'ian culture. And certainly the extensive petroglyphs above the central plain indicate a spiritual significance to this dry land. Not until after Kamehameha I unified the islands did Lana'i gain any prominence. Kamehameha favored the isolated Kaunolu fishing village and it became politically important.

Prior to 1920, *haoles* used the land to range cattle and attempted and failed at sugarcane production on the east coast. In 1922 James Dole bought 98 percent of the island and began to grow pineapple using imported Filipino labor. Beginning in the 1970s, pineapple also became economically unfeasible due to cheaper labor elsewhere and the island was returned to range land. Recently the Nature Conservancy has been gaining a greater presence on this small island as more acreage is returned to cow-free wild lands.

As you will soon find out, services on Lana'i are highly concentrated in Lana'i City and at Manele Bay. In fact, there are no services outside of these two areas with the exception of a private snorkeling day-resort at isolated Halepalaoa Landing on the far eastern shore. Nearly everything you need can be found on the periphery of Dole Park in the center of town.

If the long tropical nights get too long for you, consider staying in town for a movie at the old theater. If you have good lights on your bike, the ride back to Manele is safe enough. Moonlight makes the ride back down to the sea a ghostly experience you'll not soon forget.

There are about 30 miles of paved highway on Lana'i and most of the attractions lay beyond these avenues. A good wide-tired bike will serve you well here. Although many of the dirt roads are in excellent condition, I believe that a road bike might take all of the fun out of exploring this wild landscape.

A mountain bike would be ideal; however, my hard-tired hybrid performed well enough.

Those white passenger vans that pass you on the climb out of Manele Bay are on their way to the Resort at Koele, located 0.8 miles north of the

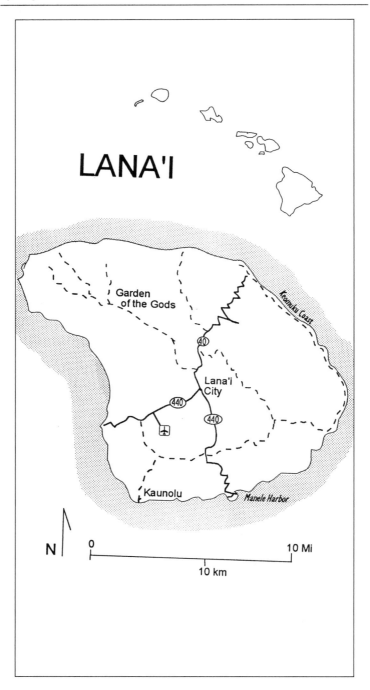

center of Lana'i City on the Keomuku Highway 44. The Resort at Koele has been nominated to Condé Nast's Top Ten resorts in the world several times in recent years. Its authentic Plantation-style elegance is charming, and formal gardens a joy. The gracious employees at Koele were nonplussed at my ragged condition after a day in the saddle. Rather, they were openly welcoming even though they must have known that I was not a guest.

An additional pleasure found in cycle touring Lana'i is that after two days every driver in Lana'i City knows you and returns waves to you on the road. After a week, you are almost family.

Getting There

There are two ways to get to Lana'i you can fly, or you can take the ferry from Lahaina. Air fares from Honolulu are about $80 each way plus $50 for your bike each way. This is reduced if you are flying continuously from the mainland (without an overnight in Honolulu). Due to a lack of demand, flights are infrequent and connections with islands other than Oahu are difficult.

The Lana'i Expeditions ferry, on the other hand, makes 5 round trips per day between Lahaina, Maui, and Manele Harbor on Lana'i. The round trip fare is $70 plus $10 each way for your bike. The boat makes its first trip from Lahaina at 6:45 A.M. and makes its last 45 minute trip back from Manele Harbor at 6:45 P.M.. Make reservations at Expeditions: (808) 661-3756, 658 Front St., Suite 127, Lahaina, Hawaii 96761. The boat leaves from the Public Landing slip in Lahaina Harbor.

Camping

Official camping is available only at Hulopoe Beach Park at Manele Bay. The Park is owned and operated by the Lana'i Company, Inc. You can reach them at (808) 565-8232. Call for reservations then send them your check for $5 each night and a $5 one-time processing fee. Their address is P.O. Box 310, Lana'i City, Hawaii 96763: Att: Camping Permits. There are only five official campsites available so reserve early. The last time I was there, there were Boy Scouts camped all over the park, and in four days no one asked to see my permits. You could probably sneak by in a pinch.

Hulopoe Beach is a gorgeous place with a long white sand beach and high sea cliffs nearby. Spinner dolphins frequent the Bay which is also a wildlife refuge. More than a few folks have swam with these gentle creatures.

The park also offers two sets of clean restrooms and three open-roofed, enclosed showers with passive solar heating if you shower early enough in the day.

Wild camping is forbidden, but so long as you're not on a small landowner's beach on the east coast, I doubt anyone would ever know or care.

Other Accommodations

There are several B & Bs available. "Dreams Come True" rentals at (808) 565-6961 has doubles starting at $75. Consult any good guide book or try the visitor information bureau: Destination Lana'i at P.O. Box 700 Lana'i City, Hawaii 96763, (565-7600) for more.

Groceries

There are three good grocery stores, all in Lana'i City, and within a few blocks of each other on Eighth Street just off Lana'i Avenue. The two largest are nearly next door to each other across from the Park. For a modest selection of Natural Foods try Pele's Garden at 811 Houston Street, closed Sundays. And that's all there is.

Restaurants

The Blue Ginger Cafe offers standard cafe fare during normal meal times, closed otherwise. The Hotel Lana'i serves reasonably priced meals all day just off Lana'i Avenue. If you're just not spending enough money, both The Lodge at Koele 1 mile north of Lana'i City and the Resort at Manele Bay, a five-minute walk from the campground, can delightfully lighten your wallet and please your palate.

Other Services:

Almost all available services are near to or border Dole Park in the center of town. There is a movie theater, Laudromat, variety store, hospital, and post office as well as a police station at Eighth and Frazier (911 works here).

Manele Campground—Kaunolu—Lana'i City

This ride makes a great introduction to Lana'i; the hills are big, the dirt roads in good shape, and you'll get to preview the other rides covered in this chapter. After a stiff 3.5-mile climb up to the caldera rim on a fine, paved road, you turn west and trace the rim of this old volcanic cauldron on a good earthen road. The road is easily ridden on wide tires, slicks or nobbies; however, thick dust would pose a bit of a challenge for the hard, narrow tires of a road bike.

Signage is especially bad on Lana'i where the economy had been focused on the now-bankrupt pineapple industry rather than tourism. Watch your mileage guide and odometer carefully to avoid unexpected "adventures."

After several miles of black-plastic-sheet studded dirt road the route sweeps down to historic Kaunolu. Once a small fishing village, Kaunolu gained importance when Kamehameha chose it as one of his favorite summer retreats. Now a wonderful self-guiding trail takes the visitor past ruins of houses, temples, storage buildings, and petroglyphs. Allow an hour to walk down to and an hour to walk out of the site. Set aside an additional hour to tour the village site itself. I was offered rides in jeeps in both directions without any effort on my part. An experienced mountain biker on the proper off-road bicycle could certainly enjoy riding this vigorous side trip.

From the junction with the road down to Kaunolu, the route rejoins paved road near the Lana'i Airport and continues on to Lana'i City where you can find pretty much whatever you need.

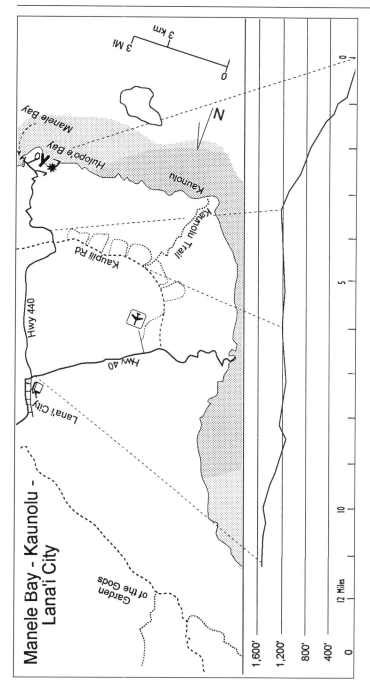

Manele Bay - Kaunolu - Lana'i City

Miles from Manele	*Miles from Lanaʻi City*
0.0	*12.9*

Begin the ride at the Manele Beach Park.

0.3
12.6
Intersection of access roads to the boat harbor and to the campground. The sign indicates the beginning of State Highway 440. Begin a 3.2-mile, 1,200-foot climb that will take you to the broad level caldera of central Lanai.

0.6
12.3
Climb past the turn-off to Manele Bay Resort. This is the last green grass you'll see for several miles in this near-desert environment.

0.8
12.1
A Wooden sign indicating 7 miles to Lanai City. As you continue this climb be certain to stop under the occasional acacia tree and watch the view unfold below you. This hillside reminds me more of Baja Mexico than of Hawaii.

3.4
9.5
Top of the hill at 1,240 feet. At the very summit there are red-dirt roads leading to both sides of a light-colored concrete patch in the asphalt highway. Up the hill to the right is the beginning of the climb up to Lanaihale, the high point on the island. To the left is the road to Kaunolu. The "road" looks more like a large, flat clearing than anything else. Go left here.

3.5
9.4
Cross a new asphalt road that leads down to the service area of the Manele Bay Resort. Continue straight ahead. Our red-earth road becomes more obvious as it leads away following the nearby rim of the caldera.

5.7
7.2
The road points directly at a white navigational beacon on the hill ahead then curves gently to the right at mile 5.8.

5.9
7.0

Turn left. Two parallel roads line a gully leading down to the left. Take the right-hand road. This surface is inferior to the good earth road above so ride with caution watching especially for deep, soft dust that can grab tires and send them in unpredictable directions.

Bear right as the road reaches the bottom of the hill.

6.7
6.2

A well-used road leads down to the ocean and to Kaunolu to the left here, but it is poorly marked. Watch for brown wooden posts on either side of the Kaunolu Road meant to be sign posts. Just west and beyond Kaunolu Road there is a large dump of white plastic pipe. If you see this, you're just past the road.

The trip down to Kaunolu is just over 3 miles long and the road is very rough, only enjoyable on a pack-free mountain bike. However, the ruins of the village are worth the hike if you're interested in such things.

7.6
5.3

Rejoin the main earth road. Turn left here to continue on to Lana'i City. Turn right to retrace your route to Manele Campground.

8.3
4.6

Over this small rise and you get a great view of northern Lana'i and west Moloka'i in the distance.

8.6
4.3

Turn right up the lesser-used road towards a large pyramidal earthen berm (the elevated southern end of the Lana'i Airport runway).

9.3
3.6

Bear left towards the strange-looking pyramidal roofs of the Lana'i Airport.

9.7
3.2

Intersect the Airport Road. The terminal has restrooms, drinking fountains, soda machines, and air conditioning for those in need of a rest on this rigorous ride.

Turn left here to continue towards Lana'i City.

10.0
2.9

Intersect with Highway 440 West. A left turn here leads you screaming down a 4 mile-long 1,200-foot drop to the now quiet Kaumalapau Harbor, formerly used for pineapple loading. There is little of interest down there and, unless you really love to ride up really big hills, you're liable to find yourself screaming all the way back up this intense climb.

A right turn here rolls you up toward Lana'i City, 3 miles and 360 feet above you. This stretch of road was the only place on Lana'i where I encountered significant trade winds, and yes, they do blow against you.

12.9
0.0

End of route. Intersection of Highways 440 East and 440 West. Either straight or left here brings you to central Lanai City up the hill (see description of route to the Garden of the Gods). A right turn here takes you across the caldera and back to Manele Bay.

Lana'i City—Central Caldera—Manele— Luahiwa Petroglyphs

This short seven-mile ride brings you swiftly from Lanai City to the port and campground at Manele Bay. It is the busiest highway on Lana'i but to see more than ten cars is unusual. This is an especially enchanting moonlight ride back to camp after dinner and a movie in town. The four-mile-long alternate route past the Luahiwa Petroglyphs not only directs you to an ancient petroglyph field and a good view of central Lana'i, but also leads you through the last remaining productive pineapple fields on Lana'i. The alternate route follows earthen roads which are generally in very good condition unless wet. Hawaiian mud is very slick.

This mostly downhill trip from Lana'i City to the campground and harbor is all on paved roads and can be traversed in about one-half of an hour. The trip in the reverse direction takes considerably longer as it is almost all uphill; you should allow a minimum of 1 hour.

The route begins in a Norfolk pine-lined suburb below Lana'i City and quickly drops through a scene reminiscent of the wheat fields of the northern midwestern United States, with rows and stacks of hay bales.

As you break out of the pines, an alternate route to the left takes you by the Luahiwa Petroglyphs before passing near a pig farm.

After rolling down though the hayfields, the road climbs shortly and presents you with a view of the wave-fringed coast below. The islands of Kahoolawe, Maui, and Hawaii float in an incredibly blue sea beyond.

A 3.5-mile screaming dive brings you back to sea level. At the bottom of the hill the road forks left to the Harbor, and right to the campground.

Miles from Lana'i City	*Miles from Manele*
0.0	*7.5*

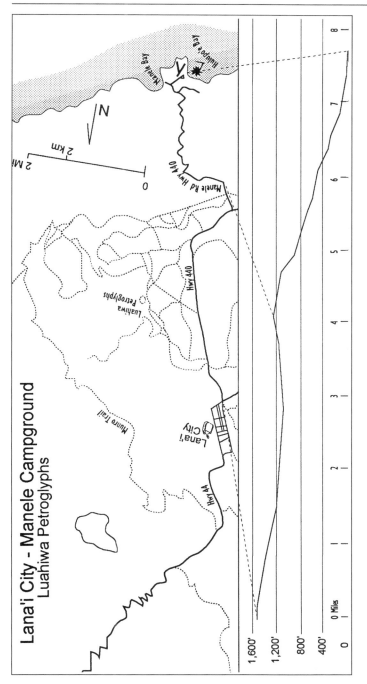

Lana'i City - Manele Campground
Luahiwa Petroglyphs

Junction of Highways 440 East, 440 West, and Highway 44 just south of Lana'i City. Head south on Highway 440 East.

0.2
7.3
Begin a delightful downhill stretch dropping 335 feet in the next 1.3 miles.

0.7
6.8
Pass two large man-made depressions on the left, formerly used as water reservoirs. The earth road at the end of the second basin leads to an intriguing petroglyph field (see alternate route at the end of this route log).

From this highland you get a good view of the central caldera. Former pineapple fields now sprout hay bales for a relatively small number of cattle. What a shame to turn this huge parcel of tropical island into something resembling central Texas.

1.5
6.0
Pass a straight, wide gravel road which leads off diagonally to the left towards a pig farm glistening in the distance.

The alternate route past the petroglyphs rejoins the Highway here.

2.9
4.6
The low spot in the caldera and the long straight in the road give way to a right-hand curve and begins to climb gently back up to the caldera rim. Elevation 1,120 feet.

3.7
3.8
An intersection with the new paved road down to the Manele Resort. Turn left up the hill.

4.1
3.4
1,230-foot elevation at the rim again. From here the road drops to sea level through 3.4 miles of sharp curves and great views. There is usually traction-destroying loose gravel on the road, especially on the corners. Resist the temptation to speed brakeless down this descent at least the first time.

7.2
0.3
The bottom of the hill. The boat harbor is to the left and the campground is 0.3 miles to the right.

7.5
0.0
Manele Bay Campground. End of route.

Alternate route

Alternate route to the Luahiwa Petroglyphs.

From Mile 0.7
From Mile 1.5

0.0
4.1
Turn on to a red-earth road at the southern side of a crater-like dry reservoir. The road starts out bad but soon gets smooth. Follow the road as it hugs the base of the bluff to the east.

1.8
2.3
Take the middle of the 3 branches here. It is less used and a little longer but maintains elevation as the caldera floor begins to drop away beneath you.

2.0
2.1
Cross a large water line before dipping into a deep gully.

2.2
1.9
Pass below a large black water tank.

2.3
1.8
Pass above a pump station with several transformers and powerlines.

2.4
1.7
Stop. Amongst the really big century plants above you are some really big boulders. Dis is dah place. Dismount and make your way through the roadside grasses and begin to scramble up the slope. The glyphs are not easy to see at first. They are old enough that the areas where the patina was scraped from the rocks are themselves becoming weathered. When I was there last, the hillside had recently burned which made navigation easier, but also charred these fascinating designs.

This is certainly one of the most dramatic views of central Lana'i and is a fine place to watch the sun set in the company of these ancient and sacred stones.

Alternate route cont.

2.6
1.5
Turn right down to the lower road and then continue left as you cross and parallel the water line.

3.2
0.9
A major intersection of dirt roads. A hard right here will take you back to Highway 440 East.

4.1
0.0
Intersection with Manele Highway. Turn left to Manele Bay and right to Lanai City. Rejoin the Lana'i City-Manele route guide at 1.5 miles from Lana'i City.

Lana'i City—Garden of the Gods

This short 15.8-mile round-trip begins with a journey through Lana'i City, past the venerable Lodge at Koele Resort, then rolls gently over the west caldera floor past grazing cows on a fine, hard-earth road. Finally you tour a cattle-excluded area populated by an otherworldly ironwood pine grove followed by an area featuring native foliage to give you an idea of what all of Lana'i originally looked like before suffering the ravages of pineapple plantations and stock grazing.

At the high point of this gentle slope you encounter the Garden of the Gods, actually an erosional badland of soft, red volcanic deposits littered with irregularly shaped, harder remnant stones. The effect of this striking badlands is amplified by years of passers-by piling the stones into cairns that would fit well in a Dr. Suess illustration. The Garden itself is augmented by a spectacular view of the entire south coast of nearby Moloka'i.

Polihua Road continues on another 5 miles, dropping 1,690 feet to windswept and desolate Polihua Beach. Beyond the Garden of the Gods the road becomes very rough and is suitable only for full-blown, pack-free mountain bikes. Extremely strong currents offshore make swimming part way to Taiwan a likely prospect.

Return the way you came with a slight short-cut variation at the end to avoid a roughly graveled climb up to Koele. This is a pleasant one-hour ride both ways. You can avoid the occasional dust-generating automobile by traveling early in the day

Miles from Lana'i City	*Miles from the Garden*
0.0	*7.9*

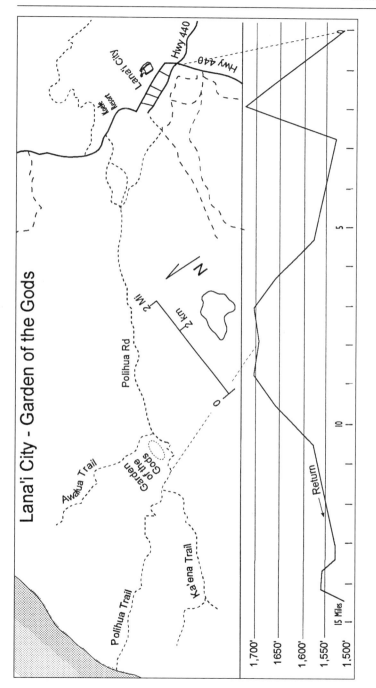

Lana'i City - Garden of the Gods

Hwy 440

Hwy 440

Lana'i City

lodge Resort

Awalua Trail

Polihua Rd

Garden of the Gods

Polihua Trail

Ka'ena Trail

N

2 Mi

2 km

0

1,700'
1650'
1,600'
1,550'
1,500'

Return

0

5

10

15 Miles

Begin at the junction of Highways 44, and 440 East and West. Head up the hill to the north on Keomuku Highway.

0.2
7.7
Turn left on Lana'i Avenue.

0.7
7.2
Pass the Lana'i City Post Office with a very interesting bulletin board covering local events and interests.

1.1
6.8
Pass a small Community Center building with fresh water available.

1.5
6.4
After the road bends right and climbs a short hill, pass the entrance to the Lodge at Koele Resort.

1.8
6.1
Turn left at the large rock displaying a sign directing you to the Garden of the Gods and pass the Koele tennis courts and stables. The gravel surface is a bit treacherous for hard tired bikes, use caution down the hill.

2.6
5.3
Turn right following the signs to the Garden. The road now becomes good packed earth as you glide through the northern Lana'i caldera. From an elevation here of 1,535 feet, climb 235 feet gently over the next 4.3 miles.

6.0
1.9
Game Management Area Sign. A large portion of northern Lana'i is under cooperative management with the Nature Conservancy. Perhaps a higher use of the land can be found than grazing cattle.

There are many branch roads in the next 2 miles and the way is often confusing. Generally the side roads are named at junctions, and the road to The Garden is the unsigned main road. If you find yourself dropping steeply toward the sea, STOP. You've taken the wrong road.

Enter a way cool weeping pine forest followed by more game management area. This cow-free area has abundant and diverse vegetation. Watch for partridge and native Nene geese.

7.9
0.0
Enter the Garden of the Gods.

Polihua Road continues on another 5 miles dropping 1690 feet to windswept and desolate Polihua. The road is very rough beyond this point. Return the way you came to Lana'i City.

On the return trip at 5.3 miles from The Garden where before you had come down from the Lodge, go straight instead to take a shortcut around the slick, gravel-paved hill-climb.

After 0.3 miles turn left uphill towards town.

After an additional 0.4 miles bear right. Pavement begins after another 0.1 miles.

0.5 miles further on the pavement becomes Frazier Street which parallels Lana'i Avenue.

0.6 miles later Frazier Street takes you by the other end of the park at the city center, and in another 0.5 miles Frazier Street intersects with Highways 440 West and East.

Munro Trail—Manele Bay to Lana'i City

This is by far the most spectacular ride on Lana'i, and like most rides on Lana'i, it is vertically challenging. This ride is 18 miles from the Manele Campground to Lana'i City, and very little of this is flat. Along the way you'll gain awesome views of Lana'i from the summit ridge as well as neighboring islands. Along the summit ridge you'll experience exotic pines and wild turkeys, see an ancient battleground, and test your dirt road riding skills. If you're on slick tires as I ride on, you'll probably also get to walk up a few really steep pitches. This is another of those rides that will stay with you for a very long time.

Like many of the roads on Lana'i, the Munro Trail, which follows the summit spine of the island, is unpaved. This ride can be characterized as somewhere between a torturous misadventure on one hand and a thrilling wilderness trek on the other. The two determining factors are your state of mind and your state of conditioning.

First and foremost, don't do this trip if it's raining on the mountain. Not only is Hawaiian mud especially treacherous stuff, but you won't be able to see anything. To avoid the latter peril, make this trip early in the day before the persistent clouds form over the summit. If there is a cloud cap above when you get to the lip of the caldera, consider rescheduling this ride.

From the Manele Bay Campground you climb up the paved road rising to the caldera rim at 1,230 feet above sea level. At the top of this climb you turn onto a well-used, but not necessarily well-maintained earth road. As you thread your way through a labyrinth of ranch roads to the southern base of the Hale ridge, you gain 700 feet in elevation and a fine view of the caldera floor below. Then the real climbing begins.

In a series of stair-step ascents, you climb 1,300 feet in 2.3 miles. Many of these "hills" are so steep that without knobby tires, spinning wheels will likely force you to walk up at least part of the way.

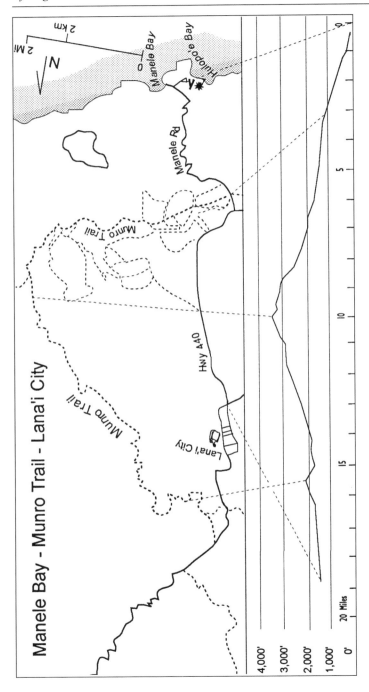

Manele Bay - Munro Trail - Lana'i City

You are rewarded with wondrous views of the other nearby islands and the extremely arid windward slopes of Lana'i to the east, and a precipitous drop to the caldera on your right. Also, as you climb, the forest becomes thicker, taller, and wetter, progressing from ironwood and *koa* to fragrant stands of eucalyptus and finally the large Norfolk pines visible from the plain below. Also watch for wild turkey, axis deer, and hunting eagles.

From Lanaihale (the summit) you can, on a good day, see all of the other major Hawaiian islands except for far-off Kauai. The descent road along the north ridge is more sparsely vegetated and the views are not so spectacular. The road itself is challenging with steep drops and some incredibly slick muddy patches. To add a last barb, the road drops to 1,700 feet in elevation before steeply climbing 300 feet to a paved road. A short downhill connects with Keomuku Road which glides south down into Lana'i City where you can reward yourself with any of the comforts of civilization you choose.

In case you weren't counting, that's a gross elevation gain of over 3500 feet. Riders enjoying a thrilling wilderness trek should allow a minimum of 3 hours. Those having a torturous misadventure are encouraged to retreat as soon as that realization is made.

One alternative to the descent on the Munro Trail is to backtrack 1.7 miles back down the south ridge to the well-marked and well-used Awehi Road which drops nearly 3,000 feet in a very steep 4.5-mile descent to Kahemano Beach. The north end of the paved Keomuku Road back up to Lana'i City is 11.2 miles north on a very level, beach-hugging dirt road. See the Lana'i City-East Lana'i Coast route description for more details on this 42-mile loop.

There is no water available between Manele Bay and Lana'i City. Be certain your bottles are full before beginning.

Miles from Manele	*Miles from Lana'i City*

0.0
18.9
Manele Bay Campground. See Manele-Kaunolu Lana'i City Route for a description of this ascent out of Manele Bay.

3.4
15.5
Top the of initial climb at caldera rim. Turn right onto the very straight earth road. You are now at 1,230 feet.

4.9
14.0
A three-way junction greets you at the end of this long, straight stretch. The numerous roads in this area make directions confusing. Invariably you will want to take the most-traveled alternative. Until Mile 6.8 you want to stay just inside the caldera as the road climbs near the southeastern ridge.

Take the middle fork here and follow along the base of this small ridge for 0.15 miles.

5.0
13.9
Turn right up this short steep hill and roll over several successive ridges and gullies for 1.5 miles.

6.5
12.4
The road becomes level and straight for 0.3 miles with the ridge to your right. You are now at 1,980 feet.

6.8
12.1
Turn 90 degrees to the right for a short, dusty climb to the top of the ridge. From this point on, the route travels along the top of the ridgeline.

7.0
11.9
Across the water a great view of Kahoolawe, Maui, and even Hawaii on a clear day. The climb begins in earnest here.

7.7
11.2
At 2,350 feet, a sign for Kapoho Unit and a fine overlook of arid east Lana'i. The faint road below and to the right is the trail to Naha village, the southern terminus of the 17-mile-long eastern Lana'i beaches.

8.1
10.8
Turn off to Waiopea Beach.

Alternate route

8.3
10.6
Alternate route: Well-traveled Awehi Road leads to the right at the sign and switchbacks down five miles and 2,625 vertical feet over barren hills to the beach below. At the beach, Awehi Road connects with and then follows the coast-hugging earthen Keomuku Road for 16 miles, at which point paving resumes in the form of Highway 44. The highway then climbs 2,000 feet over six miles to meet the other end of the Munro Trail above Lana'i City. There are no services on this dry and wild alternate.

Stay left for the main route and summit. The forest becomes speckled with fragrant Norfolk pines here. Also watch for really big wild turkeys on the forests' edge.

8.6
10.3
3,050-foot elevation. The road grade eases a bit from here on.

8.9
10.0
Still 270 feet below the summit, the road becomes nearly level here with some gut-grabbing views down to the central plain.

9.0
9.9
A small radio tower to the right.

9.3
9.6
A steep little 80-foot climb.

9.5
9.4
3,330 feet at the Haalelepaakai. A false summit followed by a steep little drop to 3,285 feet.

10.0
8.9
Lanaihale, the summit at 3390 feet. YAHOO! With some effort, all of the major Hawaiian islands except distant Kauai can be see from here on a good day.

Begin a long and rigorous descent towards Lana'i City. Drop relatively slowly over the sawteeth of the summit ridge for the next 0.8 miles.

10.8
8.1
Drop 225 feet over the next 0.3 miles.

11.1
7.8
Descent eases for the next 0.9 miles.

11.8
7.1
Hookio Ridge overlook to the right. A trail here leads to an overlook of 2,000-foot deep Hauola Gulch. The ridge line displays notches used by warriors in a 1778 defense of the island against Kamehamehas' predecessor.

12.0
6.9
A series of steep little descents dot the next 1.0 mile. Drop from 2,775 feet to 2,300 feet. Watch for wet and extremely slick muddy areas.

13.0
5.9
The road levels for 0.2 miles then drops steeply through a series of sharp curves. Cliff-like gully walls occasionally present themselves at thrilling proximity to the road.

13.4
5.5
Pass a small radio tower. Drop from 2,175 feet to 1,775 feet over the next 0.7 miles.

13.6
5.3
Stay left at this junction and continue to wind steeply down through a thickening, moist tropical forest.
14.2
4.7
The road levels for 0.6 miles at 1,690 feet as it winds past an eerie erosional badlands. This is an example of what happens when the forest cover is disturbed in this area.

14.8
4.1
Climb 130 feet in 0.1 miles. I walked up this one.
15.4
3.5
After a short drop climb a 240-foot hill. This is the last of the climbs on this route as the road levels.

15.8
3.1
Junction with a service road. Stay right here.

15.9
3.0
Pavement begins near a large cemetery. To your left is a steep gravel road that descends steeply to Koele Resort. I prefer the views available on the paved route ahead to this rough-bedded shortcut.

16.2
2.7
Intersection with Keomuku Road and Highway 44. Right leads 1,940 feet down to Ship Wreck Beach (see Lana'i City—Keomuku Road Route for details). Turn left here to continue on to Lanai City. Feel the sweet kiss of good pavement as you glide down a smoothly paved ridge traverse with views of the north Lanai plain and the route to the Garden of the Gods.

17.1
1.8
A sign here directs tourists down the hill to the Garden of the Gods (see Garden of the Gods route description for details). The road leading up the hill past the golf course is the other end of the gravel road that began above just before the cemetery.

17.4
1.5
Pass the entrance to the Lodge at Koele Resort. The lodge seems to have a very low snob factor and visitors seem welcome to tour the building and the wonderful formal gardens beyond.

18.2
0.7
Downtown Lanai City on Lanai Avenue. Ninth Street is the home of a few small variety stores and the Blue Ginger Cafe. Yum. Eighth Street features two good grocery stores.

18.7
0.2
Turn right down the hill to a major intersection.

18.9
0.0
The intersection of Highways 440 East and West. End of ride.

Lana'i City—East Lana'i Coast

This tour takes you far from the civilized center of the island down a 2,000-foot descent to the windblown, kiawe-lined east coast. The 6-mile descent will likely be slowed by head-winds which happily become tailwinds on the long, dry, shadeless climb back up. Once at sea level you're likely to have over 20 miles of beach nearly all to yourself. It is nine miles to the end of the pavement; how far you go beyond, that is up to you.

Due to the infrequency of use, these beaches are a beach-comber's paradise as the sea washes up shells, fishing equipment, and the occasional fabled Japanese glass float.

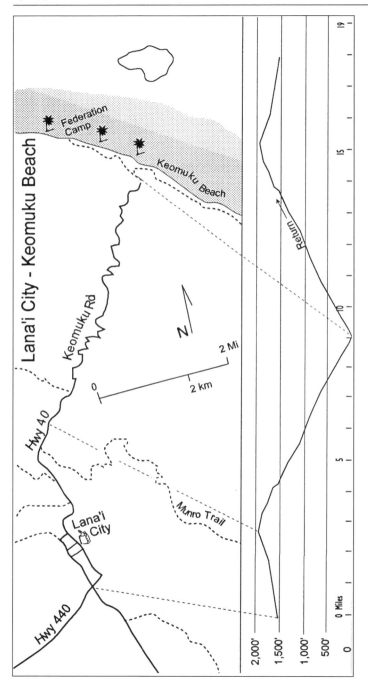

Lana'i City - Keomuku Beach

The 2-mile road to the north takes you by the ruins of Federation Camp and, beyond the foundation of a ruined lighthouse among fishing shelters, a field of distinctive Lana'ian petroglyphs. This road is made nearly impassable by deep, tire-grabbing sand, but a sunny beach hike is certainly an option.

The level dirt road to the south extends though shady *kiawe* acacia trees. Though the shade is welcome, the trees also block cooling breezes and views. They also can drop branches laden with tire-puncturing thorns, though I've not had a flat here.

The road passes several points of interest which are detailed in the route log and on the map you can pick up on the ferry boat. Most notable is the near ghost town of Keomuku. A sugar plantation center until the turn of the century, Maunalei Sugar went bust when they effectively exhausted the entire fresh ground-water reservoir under eastern Lana'i and the wells went brackish.

A loop can be made of this ride by continuing south for 11.2 wild miles down the coast road. At that point Awehi Road descends from its junction with the Munro Trail on the ridge above. The Awehi Road is passable on a good mountain bike. It is a strenuous, steep ride climbing 3,000 feet in 4.5 miles and takes you nearly to the top of the summit ridge.

If you are truly interested in braving the *kiawe* thorns of the coast road and experiencing these solitary splendors, I recommend combining the Lanaihale-Munro Trail climb with a descent down Awehi Road and returning to Lana'i City by the Keomuku Highway 44. Beginning at Manele Bay, this makes for a 42.6-mile-long loop with a gross vertical climb of about 5,000 feet. 21.4 miles of this ride is on dirt road. Allow at least seven hours of saddle time for this loop. See the Munro Trail route description for the portion leading up to the Lanaihale and the upper terminus of Awehi Road.

The alternative is to return the way you came. After your visit to this wild shore, ascend back up the well-paved and expertly-graded Keomuku Highway 44. The 6.2-mile climb takes you back up to 2,000 feet before gliding down to Lana'i City. Remember that there is no water available outside of Lana'i City and that this is likely to be a hot, dry ride. Allow one hour for the trip down to the Beach and at least two hours for the trip back up to town.

Miles from Lana'i City	*Miles from the Beach*
0.0	*9.1*

Begin at the junction of Highways 440 East, West, and South. Head up the hill to the north on Keomuku Highway. 1,525-foot elevation.

0.2
8.9
Turn left on Lana'i Avenue.

0.7
8.4
Pass the Lana'i City Post Office with a very interesting bulletin board covering local events and interests. The grocery stores are just a block away on Eighth Street.

1.1
8.0
Pass a small Community Center building with fresh water available.

1.5
7.6
After the road bends right and climbs a short hill, pass the entrance to the Lodge at Koele Resort.

1.8
7.3
Pass a large rock directing you to the Garden of the Gods and pass the Koele tennis courts and stables. 1,745-foot elevation.

2.7
6.4
Pass the junction with the road leading to the Munro Trail to the right.

2.8
6.3
Top of the hill at 1950 feet. The descent begins slowly, dropping only 300 feet in the next 1.5 miles.

3.4
5.7
Management area access road to the left at elevation of 1,850 feet.

4.3
4.8
At 1,560 feet begin a series of 9 switchbacks.

5.6
3.5
At 1,115-feet elevation the road begins a relative straight stretch dropping 260 feet in the next 0.8 miles.

6.2
2.9
The last of the Norfolk pines.

6.5
2.6
Beginning at 850 feet, 4 hairpin turns bring you 0.6 miles and 200 feet closer to the sea.

7.4
1.7
Good view of the wrecked ship hugging the coast of Ship Wreck Beach at this hard right turn.

7.8
1.3
A short straight ends with this sweeping right turn at the top of this series of 5 tight curves at 390 feet above the beach.

8.4
0.7
The 5 tight curves end here at 230 feet and are followed by 0.2 miles of gentle slope.

8.6
0.5
At 165-feet elevation, drop through the last series of turns before reaching the normally hot coastal plain.

9.1
0.0
Choices at elevation 23 feet. At this point you can walk-ride to Federation Camp to the northwest, continue 11 miles down the Keomuku coast to road's end, or sit right down and enjoy the solitude. Junction with the road to Federation Camp which departs to the left here. The Federation Camp is 2 miles away. A mile beyond the camp are the ruins of a lighthouse and just beyond that is the end of the road. To reach a group of petroglyphs, follow the Kukui Point trail for about 100 yards. This beach extends for miles, so if beachcombing is your passion, this is *da kine* place.

The right fork at this junction continues for 12.4 miles down the coast. Large acacia trees provide shade from the burning sun on this dry portion of the island.

5.7 miles down the road, Keomuku, a former cane village is nearly abandoned now.

1.2 miles beyond Keomuku on the *mauka* side is the Kahea Heiau with accompanying petroglyphs.

0.7 miles past Kahea is Halepalaoa Landing, site for day-tripping chartered dive parties from Lahaina on Maui. *Mauka* of the Landing is an old Buddhist shrine.

1.3 miles further are two *heiaus* on the *mauka* side before Lopa Gulch.

0.9 miles further is sandy Lopa Beach.

1.4 miles beyond Lopa Beach, well traveled Awehi road leaves to the *mauka* side and begins its ascent to Lanaihale.

1.3 miles beyond Awehi Road is old Naha, a former fishing site. An ancient paved trail extends along the coast and part-way up the slope above.

Mile 3.4 of the Manele Bay-Kaunolu-Lana'i City route. This concrete pad at the top of the hill, above Manele, marks the beginning of the Munro Trail, which leads over the eastern ridge in the distance, and the beginning of Kapuili Road, which leads to Kaunolu to the west.

Mile 8.9 of the Munro Trail route. A view of central Lana'i, which is 1,500 feet below, can be seen over the handlebars. At over 3,000 feet the road soon leaves the shade of the forest and enters the exposed Lana'ihale summit at 3,400 feet.

The sparsely inhabited western slope of Lana'i greets ferry travelers en route from Lahaina, Maui. Lana'ihale marks the highest point of the ridge at 3,300 feet above sea level and is traversed by the Munro Trail described in this chapter.

Chapter 5

Hawaii

Hawaii has earned the name "the Big Island," and it is a valid appellation. At just over 4,000 square miles, Hawaii has more dry land than all of the other Hawaiian Islands combined. Its twin peaks, Mauna Loa and Mauna Kea, summit above 13,600 feet above sea level. If you consider the bulk of the island that lies under water, Hawaii is the highest and most massive mountain on earth.

Hawaii's scale is not lost on the cyclist. The grand loop around the two central calderas is 230 miles long, a distance worthy of the title "touring." Unlike its smaller sisters, one loses the awareness of being on a island and gets the feeling of land under foot.

Hawaii is home to 100,000 people, yet it has the lowest population density of all the islands. 30,000 live near Hilo, 10,000 near Kona-Kailua, 2,500 in Captain Cook, and the rest are spread more thinly around these population centers. Much of the northern Kohala District and the central isthmus is thinly populated cattle country. The Parker ranch in this area is one of the largest privately held cattle ranches in the United States.

Getting There

There is regularly scheduled air service to Keahole Airport nine miles north of Kona on the west side, and to the airport at Hilo to the east. Hilo is the industrial port city on Hawaii and has the only international airport on the island. However, because sunny leeward Kona has usurped the tourist traffic, non-stop service to Hilo from the mainland has become spotty at best. If rainy Hilo is your preferred destination, ask your travel agent about flight availability. Otherwise resign yourself to arriving in Maui or Honolulu and taking a short interisland flight to either Keahole or the Hilo airport.

Names and Numbers

As with all of the islands, Hawaii uses area code 808.

The Hawaii visitors center can be reached at 250 Keawe Street in Hilo (808-961-5797)

Weather information can be heard at 935-1666, extension 1520.

There is a 24-hour eruptions advisory at 967-7977.

As with all the islands, dialing 911 will get you an emergency response. There is also a crisis line available at 969-9111.

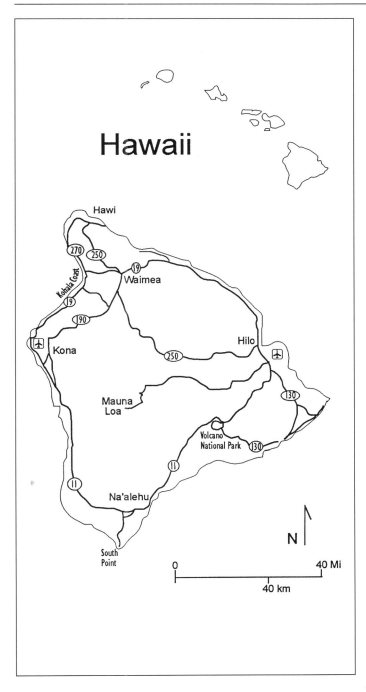

Hawaii

Hawi

270 250

Kohala Coast

19

Waimea

190

Kona

250

Hilo

130

Mauna
Loa

Volcano
National Park 130

11

Na'alehu

11

South
Point

N

0   40 Mi

40 km

Camping

Each of the following campgrounds is described in detail in the route logs. Of the publicly held campgrounds there are three administrative agencies. The County offers camping at all of the following Beach Parks: Miloli'i, Whittington, Punalu'u, Isacc Hale, Onekahakaha, Kolekole, Laupahoehoe, Spencer, Mahukona, Kapa'a, and Keokea. Each is described in its respective route log. You can make reservations for County Park camping up to one year in advance, and you can do it in person, by phone, or through the mail. Camping cost $1 per day per adult. What a deal. Contact the Park service at: Department of Parks and Recreation, County of Hawaii, 25 Aupuni Street, #210, Hilo, HI 96720 (961-8311).

The State also offers a combination of tent camping and low-cost cabin space. Cabins are offered at upland Kalopa State Recreation Area and at Hapuna Beach State Park. Tent camping is offered at MacKenzie State Recreation Area in the Puna district. Permits and reservations can be made obtained at: Division of State Parks, P.O. Box 936, Hilo, HI 96721-0936 (933-4200).

Camping in the National Park is free and requires neither permits nor reservation. Space is awarded on a first come, first served basis, however I have never seen campers turned away if there was any space available.

Other Accommodations

Each of these accommodations is described in greater detail in the route log and route introduction.

In Kailua there are a number of small condos along Ali'i Drive. Try the Kona Tiki at (808) 329-14215, P.O. Box 1567, Kailua-Kona, HI 96745.

In the uplands above Kailua-Kona there are two alternatives:

The Kona Lodge and Hostel in Honalo offers camping for $8 a night; (808) 322-9056 or P.O. Box 645, Kealakekua, HI 96750.

The marvelous old Manago Hotel in Captain Cook has some $20 singles; (808) 323-2642, P.O. Box 145 Captain Cook, Kona, HI 96704.

In rainy Hilo there are several alternatives:

Hilo Bay Inn and Hostel 311 Kalanianaole Street, Hilo, HI 96720 (808) 935-1383.

The Dolphin Bay Hotel, $40, 333 Iliahi Street, Hilo, HI 96720, (808) 935-1466.

A delightful camping alternative is offered at the Makapala Christian Center just beyond Hawi. A $3-a-night camping fee also gets you access to warm indoor showers. For information write: Makapala Christian Retreat Center, P.O. Box 129, Kapaau, HI 96745, or call at (808) 889-6271. Some dorm space available.

Camping Supplies

K-Marts and Longs Drug Stores in Kailua-Kona and Hilo can fill the more pedestrian needs of the camper. There is also C & S Cycle and Surf shop (885-5005) high up in Kamuela near Waimea. There is also The Surplus

Store in downtown Hilo at 148 Mamo Street (935-6398), and in north Kailua at 74-5617 Pawai Place (329-1240). Gaspro also has a store in north Kailua at 74-5590B Eho Street (329-7393) where you can buy gas cartridges for most stoves. Gaspro also has a store in Hilo on the way to Onekahakaha Beach Park at 525 Kalanianaole Avenue, Highway 19 (935-3341).

Groceries
Though the northern Kohala and southern Kau districts are sparsely developed, you are seldom more than 20 miles from a reliable source of groceries. Watch the route maps when in doubt. Both Hilo and Kailua have many huge grocery stores for restocking staples.

Restaurants:
Kailua-Kona offers everything from familiar fast food shops to elegant seaside dining. The old downtown section of Ali'i Drive harbors several reasonably priced, exotic eateries. Hilo also offers a full palate of tastes, the least expensive of which are downtown. Hilo is not primarily a tourist town and accordingly offers you a more utilitarian menu.

Bicycle Rental
Dave's Bike and Triathalon Shop, Kailua-Kona, (329-4522).
Hawaiian Pedals Limited, Kona Inn Shopping Village, Kona-Kailua, HI 96740 (329-2294).
Mid-Pacific Wheels, 1133C Manomo, Hilo, HI 96720 (935-6211).

Bicycle Repair
B & L Bike and Sport, 74-5576B Pawai Place, Kailua-Kona, HI 96740 (329-3309). B & L will move their full-service store to Kopiko and Palani Road, still in west Kailua, early in 1997.
The Bike Shop, 258 Kamehameha Highway, Hilo, HI 96720 (329-3309).
C & S Cycle and Surf, Kamuela-Waimea, HI (885-5005).
Dave's Bike and Triathalon Shop, Kailua-Kona, HI (329-4522).
Hawaiian Pedals Limited, Kona Inn Shopping Village, Kailua-Kona, HI 96740 (329-2294).
Mid-Pacific Wheels, 1133C Manomo, Hilo, HI 96720 (935-6211).

Kailua–Kohala
Aloha to the land of the Iron Man Triathlon. Don't be intimidated though, you don't need a will of steel to make the 52-mile ride to charming Kohala. There are two routes to Kohala, coastal and highland. This is the gentle coastal route, the highland route is described next. This route traverses 20 desert-like miles of geologically fresh lava. The verdant contrast presented by the subsequent Kohala coast is a marvelous shock. Beyond the lovely beaches and pleasant coastal detours south of Kawaihae town, the development stops, the land dries, and the coast and highway become yours to enjoy in relative solitude. Seven miles before Hawi town at the end of the route, Lapakahi State

143

Park offers an archaeologically reconstructed Hawaiian fishing village. This humble and inspiring place is full of meaning and Hawaiian spirit in a setting that is divine. Beyond the generous services of Hawi town are numerous options for accommodation. These are detailed at the end of the route log.

Kailua-Kona offers one of the highest densities of residents with hard bodies in the United States. The first-time visitor might feel that this rampant aerobic fitness might be the result of marathon shopping forays through Kailua's numerous mini-malls; or perhaps a side effect of jogging betwixt the many fine eateries offered in town. Probably not. But check out the Sibu Cafe in the Kona Banyan Court off Ali'i Drive in the heart of town to make sure.

There are numerous small hotels along Ali'i Drive, several still offer rooms, some with kitchenettes, for less than $60 a night. My favorite is the Kona Tiki at (808) 329-14215, P.O.Box 1567, Kailua-Kona, HI 96745. There is no camping officially allowed in the Kona district; however, wild camping for a night at a beach outside of town can often be successfully done.

Honokohau Beach is one place where you might camp, and you can do it in the buff if you prefer. To get there follow Highway 19 north 2.3 miles beyond the intersection with Highway 190. Turn *makai* on the road to Honokahau Small Boat Harbor. Stay right and at a blue "Beach" sign leave the road on the well-worn path. Continue past an old garbage dump to the beach. Bring water and all else that you might need, there are no services here. A little further up the beach is Honokohau National Historic Park complete with a fishpond and some petroglyphs.

While in town ask about local outdoor markets. There you will encounter locals selling produce from their own gardens. I once bought a pound of Kona coffee roasted on the spot. Yum.

The Loop to Kohala is 112 miles long and can be broken up into many smaller segments. In deciding whether to take the high road or the low road on the first leg, consider the strength and direction of the wind. Winds tend to lessen with altitude here. More importantly, consider where you want to stay. The upper Highway includes a difficult climb out of Hawi if going south, and two smaller, yet demanding climbs if heading north, yet it can be ridden in one day by a conditioned cyclist.

Appropriately, the coastal leg of this loop to Kohala follows the bike portion of the now famous triathalon event. But don't be fooled into thinking that this is a hard ride. Barring infrequent head-winds, the first 45 miles of this ride never climbs above 260 feet. Much of the land surface here is new, though, and black lava glistening in the tropical sun can create tremendous heat. As always in Hawaii, carry lots of water on this ride. And don't forget to drink it.

Miles from Kailua	*Miles from Hawi*
0.0	*51.4*

Begin in Kailua-Kona at the intersection of Highways 19, 190, and 11. Turn north on Highway 19 along the coast. Cruise above the dusty congestion of Kailua's industrial district on this well-paved, wide-shouldered highway.

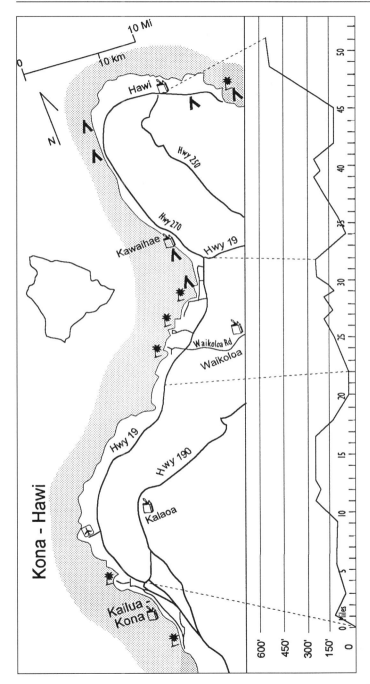

Kona - Hawi

2.3
49.1
Turn *makai* (towards the ocean) on the road to Honokahau Small Boat Harbor to reach Honokahau nude beach and unofficial camping spot. Stay right and at a blue "Beach" sign thenleave the road and follow a well worn path to the beach. There are no services here.

7.0
44.4
Busy little Keahole airport stretches on the coastal lava shelf below you. Remember, if you ever need water or other basic services, airports offer such things. Air conditioning, too.

9.0
42.4
The road swings a little closer to the coast. The land is so young here and around much of Hawaii that sand beaches and the coral reefs that protect them from vigorous wave erosion haven't yet evolved.

11.0
40.4
Top of a small rise at 260 feet before gently dropping and rising back up to 260 feet. Watch for views of far-off Maui ahead of you.

17.3
34.1
A beautiful view of the coast below. On a clear day the mountains can be seen rising behind you, and the road along the coast stretches before you for miles. Along the coast here the observant cyclist can discern several small beaches fringed with palms. These are all sites of private estates, many owned by famous people whose hired help will not be happy to see you. Don't waste your time riding down the many small roads toward the beach. The Waikoloa Beaches await you 6 miles ahead.

23.4
28.0
Alternate route: A *makai* turn here begins a 4- mile beach loop road past the Waikoloa Resort area and beautiful Anaehoomalu Bay Beach Park. Though the palm-lined beach is shared with the Resort, this is still one of Hawaii's most beautiful beaches. Drinking water, fresh showers, and picnic tables are offered.

24.2
27.2
Intersection with Waikoloa Road. Turn *makai* and continue one half mile to Anaehoomalu Beach described above. Turn *mauka* (inland) to reach

the planned Waikoloa Village with a small assortment of stores and gift shops 5.8 miles above. Inland Highway 190 is 13 miles above.

25.6
25.8
Access road to Wa'awa'a point and Makaiwa Bay. This 5-mile, round-trip loop takes you past the remains of two ancient fish ponds and some lovely coast.

28.9
22.5
Alternate route: Turn *makai* here to begin a 4-mile alternative side road that parallels the highway near the shore. Turn right (north) as you approach the shore. This will add about a mile to your trip and a smile to your lip.

30.1
21.3
Turn left at the signs to Hapuna Beach Recreation area. This is my favorite walking and wading beach on the Big Island. The golden crescent is ringed by palms and backed by grass. Hapuna looks like what I always thought a tropical beach would look like. Unfortunately, swimming here is difficult with a heavy under-tow.

Picnickers are offered pavilions, tables, water, and cool showers.

There are also six rustic cabins for rent for $15 a night. While aging in the salt air, they offer marvelous sunset views and an opportunity to free yourself from the tent for one night. Wash facilities are communal and also rustic. For information contact: Hapuna Beach Services, P.O. Box 5397, Kailua-Kona, HI 96745; (808) 882-1095.

31.3
20.1
The short, 4-mile long, beach-hugging side road returns to the highway here.

Detour: Turn *makai* to reach precious Kauna'oa Beach. Don't let the Mauna Kea Resort guard house scare you away. This is a public beach and the Mauna Kea Resort is legally bound to grant access, though they only allow ten parking spaces. Showers, water, and restrooms are provided. The curious may obtain a one-hour visitors pass to the exclusive resort but there is a stiff fine for over-staying your welcome. Holders of a validated food and libation pass are welcome to stay until the money is gone.

32.2
19.2
Intersection with Highway 270. Highway 19 turns inland here and continues on to Hilo. Stay left on Highway 270 to continue along the coast to the north end of the island.

32.7
18.7
Beach access: Turn *makai* to Samuel M. Spencer Beach Park and Campground offering you a fine small park with views of Mauna Kea above a shallow bay. Fresh water, tables, acacia trees, and outdoor showers are also featured.

The newly restored Pu'ukohola *heiau* is right next door in a free-admission National Historic site. Ask the attendant about the purification ceremony performed by Keoua Kuahu'ula, Kamehameha's cousin, en route to his ritual death at Kamehameha's hand. One might say he gave an extra inch for the heiau's dedication.

33.5
17.9
Detour: Kawaihae town is *makai* here. Don't be dissuaded by the industrial-looking docks. A charming shopping district is growing as well. There is a grocery with supplies to sustain you on the long trip to Hawi 18 miles away, and a few restaurants to please the palate. Cafe Pesto is especially good, though over-priced.

The next 12 lonely miles are bounded *makai* by rocky shores and *mauka* by thorny grazing lands. Though the Highway rolls gradually up and down, there are no real hills for the next 12 miles.

44.3
7.1
Lapakahi State Historical Park. This is a marvelously reconstructed Hawaiian fishing village. The guides here are great sources of both culture and humor. Take time to sit and watch the waves and the whales from December to April, and take time to feel the spirit of the people here; this is how they lived.

44.9
6.5
Campground: Watch for the well-signed access road to Mahukona Beach County Park and Campground. Near the abandoned shipping facilities for the defunct Kohala Sugar Company, this once-busy bay now belongs to a few fishermen and you. Beware of rough surf and considerable industrial debris lining the bottom of the bay. Amenities include electified pavilions, enclosed cool water showers, and good water.

Beyond Kapa'a the Highway gradually climbs up to 550 feet at Hawi.

45.7
5.7
Campground: Kapa'a Beach County Park and Campground access road. Even quieter than Mahukona, Kapa'a's rocky shore is best used for fishing, whale watching, and contemplating the azure sea separating you from

Maui, across the strait. The restrooms are rustic, the showers removed, and the tap water dubious. Treat it if you must drink it.

51.4
0.0
Intersection with Highway 250 in Hawi town. A right (*mauka*) turn here starts you on your way to Waimea in the central isthmus of the island. End of route: The remaining 7 miles of Highway 270 present many options. Just ahead is Kohala Spirits market and the Naito Grocery lies another 1.5 miles further on in Honomakua just off the Highway on Union Mill Road. Naito's is the last chance for groceries on this dead-end road.

The Hawi Kohala District is a string of small settlements adorned with plantation-style homes. Due to the often-cool winter weather, many roofs display chimneys for wood stoves, an oddity in Hawaii. This is the birthplace of King Kamehameha, and there is considerable memorabilia about.

There are two places to camp in this northern district. Keokea Beach County Park lies on the shore near the end of Highway 270, 7 miles beyond the junction with Highway 250. This quiet grassy site offers good water, electrified pavilions, tables, and outdoor showers. It also offers leeward weather, so be prepared for a shower. Surf can be rough so use caution swimming.

The second camping alternative is at the Makapala Christian Center on Highway 270 just 5.5 miles beyond the intersection with Highway 270. At milepost 29 watch *mauka* for the Center. Patrons here are often numerous and international. The camping area is a pleasant grassy field and the $3 a night fee also gets you access to warm indoor showers. For information write: Makapala Christian Retreat Center, P.O. Box 129, Kapaau, HI 96745, or call at (808) 889-6271. There may also be some dorm space available.

Kohala—Kailua

This 60-mile ride rises steeply above Hawi town and climbs vigorously gaining 3,000 vertical feet in 12 miles. The ride throughout is lovely, views of the coast below and giant Mauna Kea and Mauna Loa ahead spring out to greet and refresh you.

If the ascent seems disheartening, remember that once this summit is topped, you get to spend a large portion of the next 45 miles gliding back down to the sea in Kailua-Kona. There are no other major climbs beyond this one.

There are groceries and services in Waimea, 21 miles from Hawi, and at tiny Kalaoa town, 50 miles from Hawi. There is little development between these two oases so supply yourself as needed. Though this used to be the only connection between Hawi and Waimea, the traffic is light, and gets even more so beyond Waimea. Enjoy this lonely, silent road.

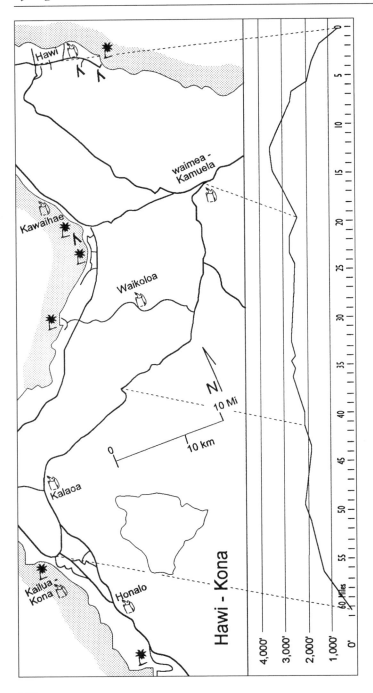

Miles from	*Miles from*
Hawi	*Kailua*
0.0	*60.3*

Begin south on Highway 250 in Hawi at the intersection of Highway 270 and Highway 250, the Kohala Mountain Road. The next services are over 20 miles ahead in Waimea. Don't leave Hawi without food, and plenty of water.

Starting at 500 feet above sea level, the Highway climbs steeply for the first 1.7 miles up to 1300 feet. Several portions of the road are lined with charming protective pines which nearly make a living tunnel. Don't forget to look over your shoulder occasionally for increasingly commanding views of Maui's 10,000-foot high Haleakala.

1.7
58.6

The grade eases slightly here, but you still have 10.6 miles and 2,300 vertical feet to go to the top of this hill. Find a comfortable gear and pace that you can maintain. There are no cookies awarded for being the first to the top of the hill. As you continue your climb watch for cactus to begin to appear in the ever-drier pastures. You'll notice that the climate is changing as you climb, becoming both cooler and drier—both are welcome changes for over-heated cyclists.

7.1
53.2

The road becomes nearly level for the next 0.8 miles before continuing the climb. You're at 2,700 feet with only 800 vertical feet to go. Makai below you the coast Highway winds along the shore.

10.1
50.2

Von Holt Memorial Park and Ironwood Avenue. This is a pleasant place for a picnic. Watch for transient rainbows on the hillside above you.

12.3
48.0

You've made it to the top at 3,500 feet above the sea. The road is almost level for the next 3.0 miles.

13.8
46.5

A viewpoint here allows you to get safely off the road while you gasp in awe at the sight of the often snowcapped Mauna Kea reaching 10,000 feet into space above you. The Kona coast stretches into the haze ahead and below as ruminating bovines fertilize the cactus in the fields.

15.0
45.3
Begin a 4.4-mile downhill thrill as you drop over 1,000 feet down to the central isthmus.

19.4
40.9
Kamuela town and the intersection with Highway 19. Turn left on 19 to continue on to Waimea.

21.4
38.9
Central Waimea and the intersection with Highway 190, the Mamalahoa Highway. There is a KTA Supermarket here in Waimea along with a plethora of smaller specialty shops and restaurants. The next services are in Kanaola town 30 miles ahead so stock up here.

When you're ready to leave town, turn onto Highway 190. The next 15 miles of road are nearly level as you roll toward the shoulder of Mauna Kea.

27.6
32.7
Intersection with the Saddle Road, Highway 200. This "short cut" to Hilo climbs an additional 4,000 feet through the high valley between Mauna Kea and Mauna Loa. Stay straight on Highway 190 as you roll past the Polo Grounds. Matches are held on Sundays.

32.4
27.9
Intersection with Waikoloa Road. A *makai* turn here brings you 13 miles down to the coast at Anaeho'omalu Beach, 24 miles north of Kailua-Kona by way of Highway 19. The carefully planned Waikoloa Village lies half-way down the hill with full services if you are in an emergency. Otherwise continue on Highway 190.

36.7
23.6
Begin a very gentle descent dropping 800 feet over the next 6.5 miles.

44.7
15.6
Begin a very gradual climb: 260 feet over the next 5 miles.

48.3
12.0
The lookout here affords a wonderful view of the Kona coast 2,000 feet below.

49.7
10.6
Slowly begin the 10-mile descent down to Kailua.

50.3
10.0
Kalaoa town, home of the Matsuyama Food Mart. They've got what you need.

56.3
4.0
Palani Junction. Highway 190 plunges to the right to Kailua 4 miles and 1,300 vertical feet below. Watch for traffic entering the Highway on this stretch.

If you are continuing south you can bypass Kailua-Kona and save yourself the effort of climbing back up to 2,000 feet by going straight on Highway 180, the Kona Belt Road. You will meet Highway 11 southbound, a level 11.2 miles ahead in Honalo town, after passing below the Kahalu'u Forest Preserve. Honalo is at mile 8.4 from Kailua on the first leg of the Big Circle route description and is home to a convenience store. Kealakekua, 0.8 miles past Honalo on Highway 11, offers two supermarkets and a hostel.

60.3
0.0
Kailua-Kona and the intersection of Highways 190, 19, and 11, the beginning of the Kailua-Kohala route. You're back where you started from. Continue straight down the hill on busy Palani Road to reach the harbor and Ali'i Drive, the heart of Kailua-Kona.

The Big Loop

At 220 miles in length, the circumference tour of the Big Island is certainly the longest tour available in the Hawaiian islands. While this route passes through the three most-developed areas on the island, there are long stretches of low population density and services can be scarce.

Though this loop is often close to the coast, there are several considerable climbs out of Kona, up to Kilauea crater in the National Park, and again up to Waimea in the central isthmus. If you don't like hills, this tour is not for you. However, the Highway is well graded and the major climbs are a day apart, so if you've trained for this ride, the hills will only make it more enjoyable for you.

Kailua—Whittington Beach

This 64-mile section takes you out of Kailua-Kona up into coffee country and the charming communities around upland Captain Cook. There are only two areas offering officially approved alternative accommodations along the way. The area around Captain Cook offers several inexpensive options. The Kona Lodge and Hostel in Honalo has camping for $8 a night;

(808) 322-9056 or P.O. Box 645, Kealakekua, HI 96750. The marvelous old Manago Hotel in Captain Cook has some $20 singles; (808) 323-2642, P.O. Box 145 Captain Cook, Kona, HI 96704. Camping is also available at Miloli'i Park Campground. Unfortunately, for the vertically resistant, Miloli'i is at the end of a spur road 1,700 feet below the Highway. It features pit toilets, no showers, and the nearby market is the only source of drinking water.

After you leave the busy environs of Captain Cook, local traffic thins and the forest thickens. The Highway belongs to you and the mongoose. Judging from the roadside casualties, one grows to doubt their reputed quickness. A few miles beyond the end of Kailua settlement the Highway traverses several lava flows extruded in the past 70 years. In decades past, several large parcels of land here were unscrupulously sold to mainlanders sight unseen as cheap, scenic vacation land. Real estate really does move on Hawaii.

Miles from	*Miles from*
Kailua	*Kohala Coast*
0.0	*189.3*

Begin at the junction of Highways 190, 19, and 11 above the center of Kailua-Kona. Head south on Highway 11, the Mamalahoa Highway. Begin a long, straight, well-graded 1,500-foot climb up to Kealakekua 9.2 miles away.

4.8
184.5

Straight through the intersection with Kamehameha III Road, Highway 185, which heads back down to Keauhoa Bay Resort area at the southern end of Ali'i Drive.

8.4
180.9

Honalo town and the intersection with Highway 180 heading north to Waimea. Continue south on Highway 11. There is a Circle K market here. You're at 1,440 feet and the top of this hill is only 0.8 miles ahead.

9.2
180.9

Kealakekua and the top of the hill. There are two large supermarkets and various other services available in this market center.

10.5
178.8

Drop back down to Captain Cook, charming home of the pink Manago Hotel, sometimes theater, and full-time restaurant featuring Lanai dining with a view of the sea far below.

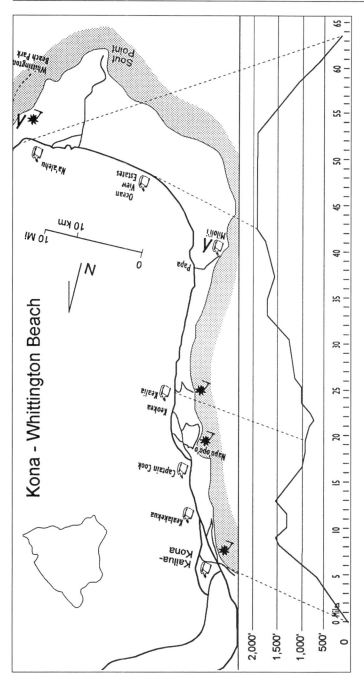

Kona - Whittington Beach

Alternate route and side trip

11.0
178.3
Alternate route

On the outskirts of Captain Cook, Napo'opo'o Road begins a roller-coaster ride 1,300 feet down to the sea. A right turn on Napo'opo'o Road can also be used as a scenic alternate route to busy Highway 11. This diversion saves you 6.5 miles of highway and a 300-foot climb.

2.6 miles along there is an intersection with Middle Ke'ei Road. A left turn here traverses the hillside 0.8 miles to the intersection with Painted Church Road. Go right here and 1.5 miles further on to the St. Benedicts' Painted Church. You will not be disappointed by a stop here. Just beyond the church the road joins Highway 160 rising up the hill from the charms of the coast below. Turn left here and follow Highway 160 one mile back to Highway 11.

Side Trip: If you don't mind riding back up the hill, the trip down to Napo'opo'o is wonderful. At the bottom of a rollicking ride down Middle Keei Road, the very swimmable Napo'opo'o Beach Park awaits you. Next to it is a well-preserved *heiau*. The Park features a picnic area, restrooms, and showers, and there is a sometimes soda stand just up the road. This is the bay, and the white monument up the coast marks the spot where Captain Cook was killed over a dispute involving the theft of a launch boat.

Follow the poorly paved Pu'uhonua Road, Highway 160, four miles south along the coast to Honaunau Bay and the Pu'uhonua O Honaunau National Historic Park. This idyllic spot was the site of the largest City of Refuge in all of Hawaii. Those who broke *kapu*, no matter what the crime, were offered sanctuary if they could just reach the gates before often-angry pursuers could catch them. Now rebuilt and restored, this site features extensive morterless stoneworks, statuary, and buildings scattered amid palms and waves. The beach under the palms here is one of my favorite lunch spots in all the world.

Follow Highway 160 up the hill above Honaunau 3.6 steep miles to rejoin Highway 11. 2.6 miles uphill, Painted Church Road leaves to the left. The church is only a few hundred yards down the road and is well worth the effort.

13.3
176.0
For those of you still on the Highway, you're at the top of this hill at 1,580 feet. Yahoo!

16.9
172.4
The steep downhill begins to level.

18.5
170.8
The road down to Napo'opo'o rejoins Highway 11 near milepost 104.

156

19.8
169.5
Kealia town. Stock up at the Fujihara Store here, the next grocery is 23 miles away in Ocean View Estates. The next 20 miles is relatively undeveloped and the road passes through successive recent lava flows. The abundance or absence of forest is an indication of the lava's youth. Much of this land surface has been extruded in the past century.

21.9
167.4
At 720 feet, this is the low spot in the Highway grade in this part of the island.

30.9
158.4
Though the road has been climbing very gently since Kealia, the grade increases slightly through the next 2.7 miles. Watch for mongoose darting in and out of the forest.

33.6
155.7
Detour: Watch for a sign directing you to a spur road *makai*. What you'll find is a narrow road which winds over fresh lava 5 miles and 1,300 vertical feet to Miloli'i, perhaps the most authentic fishing village in the State. Some folks still speak Hawaiian here as they prepare to go to sea in their dugout canoes. The nearby primitive campground offers pit toilets and a basketball court, but no water. There are lyrical sheltering ironwoods to camp beneath in this wonderfully serene place. There is also a small store in town where you can buy the basics.

38.1
151.2
Just beyond a low point in the grade, watch makai for a Macadamia nut orchard.

41.5
147.8
Manuka State Wayside and Gardens. Though there are no services available here, the wonderful garden walks warrant a short stop. The next store is just 1.5 miles ahead.

43.0
146.3
Ocean View Estates. Other than the store, there's not much of interest here. The next grocery store is 18 miles ahead in Na'alehu.

53.1
136.2
Intersection with South Point Road.

If continuing straight on Highway 11, drop 800 forest-draped vertical feet over the next five miles.

Side trip

Side Trip: The southernmost point in the United States lies 10.8 roughly paved miles and 2,000 vertical feet below. If you have the stamina, it is an unforgettable side trip. The journey to South Point begins with a pleasant glide through forest, which slowly gives way to pastures with cows and unforgettable fields of huge wind generators. Just before the parking lot for the boat launch watch for trails leading to the left. Green Sand "Beach" is about 1.5 miles along the coast. The beach is actually a volcanic crater which has been dissected by the powerful waves exposing olivine-rich cinders, which are green. The ocean is often wild here and you would be wise to marvel at it from a dry perspective.

On your way back up to the Highway, watch for Kamaoa Road on your right 9.1 miles from the boat launch. A right turn here will take you through 4 idyllic miles gently down hill to rejoin Highway 11 at Route Log Mile 58.8. This alternative route saves you the final 500 feet of climbing back up to the Highway, and about 3 miles.

58.8
130.5
Kamaoa Road to South Point joins the Highway. Watch for the world-renowned Mark Twain Monkey Pod Tree. The road frolics 500 vertical feet downward over the next 2 miles.

60.8
128.5
Na'alehu town. This is the last stop for groceries if you are staying at either Whittington Beach or Punalu'u Beach Parks. The next store is 13 miles ahead in Pahala. The water quality at Whittington Beach is questionable, so you may want to buy some extra here.

63.0
126.3
Roadside sea cliffs offer a commanding view of this short stretch of black sand beaches.

63.4
125.9
Look for a small sign to the right just past the bridge. Take a right and stay right to the bottom of the hill and Whittington Beach County Park and Campground. This tiny park has several electified pavilions, an enclosed out-

door shower, and picnic tables as well as a beautiful stand of palm trees in the middle. If the coconuts are falling, don't camp under them.

Whittington Beach—Hilo

At South Point you officially left the leeward and entered the windward portion of the island. The practical result of this is that you are no longer in the rain shadow of the central mountains and are penetrating ever further into a wet climate regime. The forest becomes more lush, and the road becomes more puddled. This southern section of the island typically receives 60–80 inches of rain each year, which is not so much when compared to the 100–150 inches which fall on the coastal hills north of Hilo.

This 61-mile segment begins with a tour of some of Hawaii's famous black sand beaches. Soon the Highway begins a well-graded and unrelenting 27-mile climb to the 4,000-foot shoulder of the still active Kilauea volcano. The popular Namakani Paio National Park Campground heralds your arrival at the summit.

The Volcanoes National Park offers immediate marvels for those too tired to explore far off the Highway, an inspiring 11-mile circle drive rims the caldera, and a 50-mile round trip to the ocean and the most likely site of active volcanism at any given time.

Remember that at 4,000 feet, even in the tropics, higher altitude means cooler temperatures, especially at night. Plan your wardrobe accordingly.

Beyond Volcano town you have a 32-mile glide back down to sea level and the principal city of Hilo. With 30,000 residents, Hilo is large enough to offer nearly any service you desire, from night life to bike shops. There is even a nearby campground.

Miles from Kailua	*Miles from Kohala Coast*
63.4	*125.9*

Begin traveling northeast at the entrance to Whittington Beach County Park. Highway 11 rolls up and down along this wild, palm-studded coast for the next 5 miles.

68.1
121.2
Beach access: The road *makai* is the first turnoff to Ninole Cove.

68.7
120.6
Beach access: Ninole Road at mile post 56. Follow the sign to the black sands of Punalu'u Beach County Park and Campground. There are lighted pavilions, cold water showers, restrooms, and good water. The only safe swimming is at Ninole Bay 0.3 miles south.

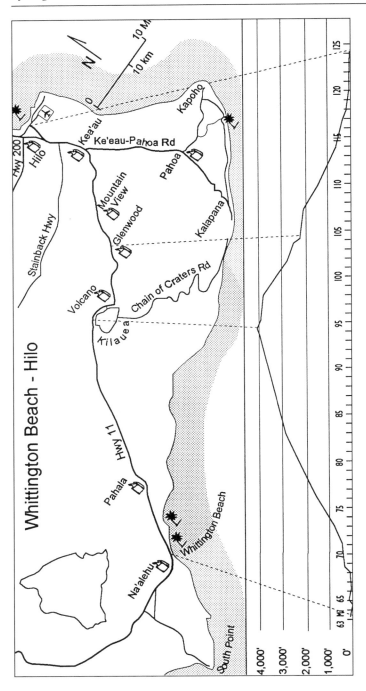

There is a minor resort at Ninole with a restaurant and some rudimentary services. There are also likely to be busloads of tourists near the restaurant trucked in to see these fabled black sands.

At this point the Highway begins a 26-mile-long ascent to 4,000 feet above sea level. The road is well graded, and this is a very long and strenuous endeavour. Pace yourself, use your gearing, drink plenty of water and take breaks. A steady, sustainable pace is your best bet.

73.2
116.1
Pahala town, site of the Mizuno Suprette. This is the last market until Volcano, 24 miles above. This is also the last store before the campground at Nanakani Paio. Buy accordingly, and be certain to have enough fluids onboard to get you to the top.

74.9
114.4
Watch for Macadamia nut orchards *makai*.

83.4
105.9
Enter Hawaii Volcanoes National Park. You're at 2,900 feet. The grade eases here as you climb the next 1,100 feet over 10 miles of road.

93.9
95.4
Near the summit watch for the well-marked entrance to Namakani Paio Campground. There is no fee, no reservation, and no permit required here. There are also no showers. There are flush toilets and plenty of good water for sluicing off the grime. The site also gets 100 inches of rain a year. Be prepared for cool, wet weather, especially November through March.

The Park concessionaire also has cabins for rent here. $35 will get you a cabin which sleeps four and the key to a communal bathhouse with hot water. Reserve far in advance at Volcano House, P.O. Box 53, Hawaii Volcano National Park, HI 96718, or call at (808) 967-7321.

93.7
95.6
Summit at 4,010 feet. Congratulations.

95.8
93.5
The entrance to the Park proper is to the right here.

Side Trip: The Volcano House Hotel is only 0.5 miles inside the Park and is a marvel of geothermal delights. There is also a fairly level 10.6-mile-long road circling the often smoldering Kilauea caldera.

The Chain of Craters Road plunges 4,000 feet down to the coast 18.2 miles away. This road once continued through to the Puna district, but recent lava flows have cut it off and it now deadends after following the coast for 6 miles. Retrace your route after checking out this steaming landscape. The Visitor Center at Volcano House can tell you how active the volcano is before you come all the way down this desolate road. There are no services on this road.

97.5
91.8
Volcano town, home of the Kilauea General Store. Begin a 25-mile downhill. You earned it.

104.5
84.8
Glenwood town. These developments are suburbs to Hilo.

107.7
81.6
Begin a steep 2-mile descent dropping almost 600 feet.

109.8
79.5
The town of Mountain View, home of a market by the same name and a real live bakery. Indulge.

116.8
72.5
At 1,400 vertical feet, Kea'au town offers a full range of services including Kea'au Natural Foods and The Filipino Foods Store.

Side Trip: Highway 130 leads to the right here giving access to the Puna district from which Highway 130 is the only exit. Pahoa town provides full services 11.5 miles along the way. From Pahoa a circle route begins to the right on Highway 130 which climbs over an 1,100-foot pali before descending to the shore, 8.3 miles from Pahoa. Continuing south 3.5 miles brings you to the north side of that road-munching lava flow from Kilauea. A U-turn and continuation down the coast-hugging Highway 137 brings you 11 miles past numerous *heiaus* and beaches to Pahoa-Pohoiki Road, which will take you the 7.5 miles back up to Pahoa. Neither MacKenzie State Recreation Area, nor Isacc Hale Beach County Park and Campground offers water, showers, personal safety, or much of anything else.

120.4
68.9
Enter the outskirts of Hilo.

124.2
65.1

Intersection of Highway 11 with Highway 19 going north. This busy intersection is near Hilo's industrial harbor and just west of the Hilo International Airport. Downtown is 1 mile to the left.

There is camping available in Hilo. From this busy intersection turn right on Kalanianaole Avenue, also known as Highway 19. Continue on for 2 miles as you pass the airport. Watch for Onekahakaha Beach County Park and Campground. There are full amenities including drinking water and showers. This urban park comes complete with a contingent of native squatters (don't be intimidated and don't be disrespectful), and a semi-natural solar-heated ocean water swimming pool.

Hilo also offers two extraordinary roofed accommodations. There is the Hilo Bay Inn and Hostel in the old Kuhio Gardens next to the sea, dorm bunks for around $20; 311 Kalanianaole Street, Hilo, HI 96720 (808) 935-1383. There is also the Dolphin Bay Hotel, each room with a deep Japanese style bath and kitchenettes, all for less than $40 a night. The Dolphin Bay is just north of downtown and two blocks off the bay near Pu'ueo Park at 333 Iliahi Street, Hilo, HI 96720, (808) 935-1466.

Hilo—Kohala Coast

This 65-mile segment begins with 27 miles of quiet highway rolling gently along the Hamakua coast. This is the wet side of the island and stream-filled gullies and waterfalls rush through lush tropical forest on the way to the ocean. Though there are many small hamlets in this former cane-growing region, there is little tourist development.

At Honoka'a, Highway 19 leaves the coast and climbs into the central isthmus. At nearly 3,000-foot elevation, sprawling Waimea sits atop the isthmus and in the center of *paniolo* cattle country. Waimea offers full services from groceries and restaurants, to hotels, to golf.

Also here in Waimea you are offered a choice of several directions to take. You can turn left on Highway 190 and take an upland route back to Kailu-Kona. This route is nearly level until it begins to descend into Kailua, 39 miles away.

Or you can head north to Hawi and the Kohala district on the upland Highway 250 which leads to the right 2 miles beyond the intersection with Highway 190. From the intersection in Kamuela, this highway climbs 1,100 feet in 6 miles before diving 3,000 feet down to Hiwa town 19 miles away from Kamuela.

Or you can continue straight down Highway 19 eight miles to its junction with Highway 270 on the Kohala coast. Kailua-Kona is 32 miles south along a rolling coast Highway 19. There are numerous camping and shopping options near the end of this route at the intersection of Highways 19 and 270. For descriptions of each of these alternative routes and facilities see the Kailua-Kohala loop section.

Miles from   *Miles from*
Kailua   *Kohala Coast*
124.2   *65.1*

At the east end of Hilo's crescent beachfront, start at the intersection of Highways 19 and 11. Head west along Bayfront Highway 19. In a little over a mile, just past Shipman Street, Highway 19 becomes Hawaii Belt Road and keeps its designation as Highway 19. The next groceries are just 12 miles ahead in Honomu.

127.2
62.1
Hilo finally ends and the land becomes far less inhabited.

130.0
59.3
Papa'ikou County Park.

130.6
58.7
Alternate route: 0.6 miles beyond Papa'ikou Park the 4-mile-long Pepe'ekeo Scenic Drive takes you on a sinuous, vine-draped, waterfall-be-sprinkled portion of the old Highway. This alternate will add a little time to your trip, but you're not here to have a fast vacation, are you?

133.4
55.9
The Highway climbs to 530 feet here then begins to roll back towards the beach.

33.8
55.5
Pepe'ekeo Scenic Drive re-enters the Highway.

136.6
52.7
Honomu town. Jan's Market offers you refreshments. The next market is 11 miles ahead.

Side Trip: Watch for the signs directing you *mauka* to Highway 220 and Akaka Falls State Park. The parking lot lies 3.5 sugarcane-lined miles up the hill. For your efforts you will be rewarded with a 40-minute walk through forests draped with wild orchid, giant red-tipped ginger, and darkly mysterious bamboo stands. Along the way you are treated to two separate waterfalls. Akaka, the higher of the two, drops 420 feet in a single cascade.

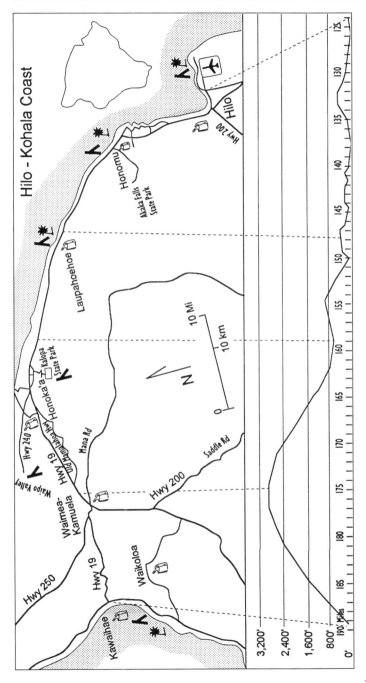

Hilo - Kohala Coast

137.4
51.9
Kolekole Beach County Park and Campground. The Park offers a black sand beach with frequently powerful surf, open air showers, and water of dubious quality. 30 inches of rain in a month is not uncommon here during the winter.

147.7
41.6
Laupahoehoe town is a pretty little place with a full service grocery store. There are supermarkets 17 miles ahead in Honoka'a.

149.2
40.1
Beach access: Laupahoehoe Road to Laupahoehoe Beach County Park and Campground. Watch for a right turn *makai* just after the bridge, then right again by some very nice homes to the Park. There are open-air showers and good drinking water. There is also a Memorial to a group of school-children drowned here in a tsunami in 1946.

151.2
38.1
Begin a 3.5-mile, 700-foot ascent.

154.7
34.6
Summit of this grade at 920 feet. Descend back towards the sea over the next 4.5 miles.

158.2
31.1
Pa'auilo town. Get camping permits here for Waipio Valley.

159.1
30.2
Time to climb again, only this time Pele means business. Waimea town awaits you 20 miles ahead and 2,300 feet above.

162.0
27.6
Side Trip: *Mauka* turn up to Kalopa State Recreation Area. The 3-mile trip climbs 1,300 vertical feet up into the forest and makes for a delightful trek. Once there you will find a truly Hawaiian forest. For several years, volunteer groups have removed all non-native species, leaving only those plants that were able to colonize and evolve in exquisite isolation in these remote Hawaiian islands.

You will also find several small cabins with hot showers tucked away in this cool, damp forest. Rates are on a sliding scale with the cost per person decreasing as the number in your party increases. Prices start at $8 per person, $12 for two people. For information contact: State of Hawaii, Division of Parks, 75 Aupuni Street, Hilo, HI 96721-0936, (808) 933-4200.

164.2
25.1
With 2,000 inhabitants, Honoka'a offers a full range of services including a Stop and Shop and a K & K supermarket. Waimea is still 1,700 feet above and 15 miles beyond, so stock up. Highway 19 changes its moniker at this point from the Hawaiian Belt Road to the Mamalahoa Highway.

Side Trip: Waipio Valley. A right turn onto Highway 240 takes you on a lush 9.3-mile 800-foot climb to the end of the road at a 2,000-foot precipice overlooking the beautiful emerald Waipio Valley. Inhabited and carefully cultivated for over a thousand years, and finally abandoned after the last tidal wave in the 1940s, Waipio offers free camping amid the remnant fields and orchards. The road down to the valley floor is traversed daily by sight-seeing tour jeeps, but it is 2,000 feet down and it is a rough road suitable only for mountain bikes. There are no services in the valley, though there is a refreshing river to swim in. Permits are required, but seldom checked. Get one from the Hamakua Sugar Company Office next to the post office in Pa'auilo town, 6 miles south of Honoka'a on Highway 19.

165.2
24.1
One mile beyond the junction of Highway 19 with Highway 240, the road begins a relatively steep 2.6-mile-long, 650-foot pitch.

167.8
21.5
The grade relaxes slightly. Climb another 650 feet over the next 3.7 miles.

174.9
14.4
The summit at 2,900 feet, 1.0 miles past the intersection of Highway 19 with the Old Mamalahoa Highway. If the weather is clear, you can see the often-snowcapped Mauna Kea to your left towering 10,700 feet above you. Development begins to sprawl as you approach Waimea.

179.3
10.0
Continue straight through the center of Waimea town; it is marked by the intersection of Highway 19 with Highway 190 South to Kailua-Kona. This relatively level route winds 30 miles along the shoulder of Mauna Kea

before beginning a 10-mile descent to Kailua. See the Hawi-Kailua Route description for details.

181.3
8.0
Continue straight past the intersection with Highway 250 North to Hawi and the charming North Kohala district. See the Kailua-Kohala Loop description for further details.

Highway 19 drops 800 feet over the next 4 miles of straight road.

185.3
4.0
Highway 19 begins a series of curves and the grade steepens. The ocean rushes up to greet you as you fall 1,300 feet over the next 4 miles.

189.3
0.0
Intersection with Highway 270 North to Hawi. Kawaihae town with restaurants and services is 1.2 miles to the right. Also to the right is Spencer Beach County Park and Campground. Hapuna Beach State Park is 2.1 miles to the left (south) on Highway 19. Kailua-Kona is 32 miles to the south along the coast. See the description of the Kailua-Kohala Loop for more details about this marvelous area.

In the highlands of the central isthmus, rainbows are often fleeting as windward clouds quickly dissipate in the drying eastern air.

Chapter 6

Kauai

Kauai is also known as the Garden Isle. Perhaps its strongest claim to that title is the fact that it is the only major island without a large dry, desert-like area. On Kauai you can be rained on just about anywhere. In fact, the Alakai swamp on the 4,000-foot summit table-land is the consistently wettest place on earth with an average rainfall of 450 inches.

If you go to Kauai before the year 2000 you will likely hear about Hurricane Iniki which struck the island in 1992 and serves as a backdrop for all the recent "rebuilding." Fact is those eager beavers have long surpassed the rebuilding point and have launched full speed into over-building. The area from Lihue and Waimea is rapidly becoming a continuous development zone. Unless you fantasize about how much fun you would have as a Manhattan Bike Messenger, you should avoid riding this portion of the highway near rush hour. Its safe, it's just not fun.

There is no complete circle road around Kauai, so all rides are there and back. From the airport in Lihue, Highway 56 rolls along the low shoulder of eastern Kauai for 38 miles to the end of the road and the east end of the Na Pali coast. West of Lihue, Highway 50 curves along the west coast for 38 miles to the end of the road at Polihale State Park and the western end of the Na Pali coast. On the way to Polihale you can turn *mauka* and climb the 4,000 feet over 20 miles to the end of the road in Koke'e State Park.

Water-guzzling sugarcane is still in production on Kauai's broad lowland shoulders. However, if the recent death of the industry on Hawaii and Oahu are any indication, sugar cane may open the broad red slopes to a less onerous ecology.

Getting There

There are no direct flights to Kauai from the mainland. However, there are numerous flights from Honolulu as well as other islands. Check with your airline or agent for details. Interisland flights generally cost from $60 to $110 each way. The 95-mile flight from Honolulu takes about 25 minutes. Mahalo and Aloha Air are the two primary carriers.

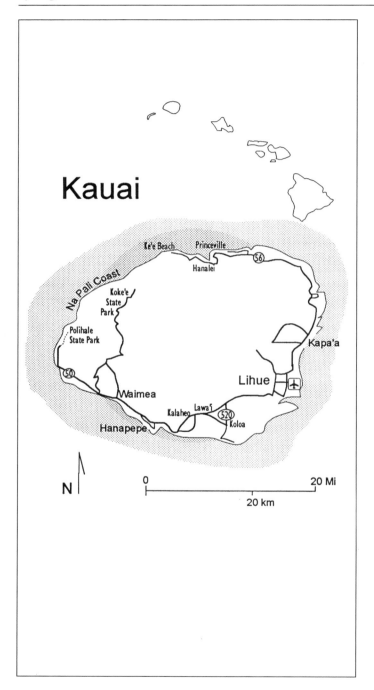

Kauai

Ke'e Beach · Princeville
Hanalei
Na Pali Coast
Koke'e State Park
Polihale State Park
56
Kapa'a
50
Lihue
Waimea
Kalaheo · Lawa'i
520 · Koloa
Hanapepe

N

0   20 Mi
20 km

Names and Numbers

As in all the islands, the area code is 808.

911 works for calling for emergency help. There are also two crisis hotlines at 245-7838 and 245-3411.

The Visitors Information Bureau can be reached at the Lihue Plaza Building, 3016 Umi Street, #207 Lihue or call toll free 1-800-AH-KAUAI (245-3971). Write them at P.O. Box 507, Lihue, HI 96766 for a free illustrated map and other goodies.

In the past three years Kauai has greatly expanded local bus service and it is now possible to bus nearly anywhere on the island for $1, although there are some complaints about slowness of the system. Phone 241-6410 for information.

24-hour recorded weather information at 245-6001.

Camping

For a complete description of each camping area, see the three route logs for Kauai.

The Kauai County Parks Department maintains seven campgrounds around the periphery of the island (Niumalu Park near Lihue was closed at press time). There is a charge of $3 per night per person. Reservations can be made by contacting the Permits Office at: 4193 Hardy Street, Lihue, HI 96766 (245-8821). You can also obtain permits directly from rangers on site or from the police station in Lihue at 3060 Umi Street for $5.

The State maintains three bike-accessible Parks. Polihale sits alone and lovely at the western terminus of the ring road, and Ha'ena Beach Park, beautifully situated but tired of the attention, lies near the eastern end of the ring road. Koke'e Park lies high on the western shoulder at nearly 4,000 feet and has some cabins for rent. For free State Parks Permits contact the Division of State Parks, 3060 Eiwa Street, #306, Lihue, HI 96766 (241-3444).

Other Accommodations

Busy YMCA Camp Naue lies near Ha'ena State Park beyond Hanalei. They offer $10 camp sites and $12 bunks and warm showers. Contact them at: P.O. Box 1786, Lihue, HI 96766 (246-9090). Call before you go.

Nestled in foothills and backdropped by the dramatic vertical green curtain of the uplands, and six miles west of Lihue, Kahili Mountain Park offers cabins starting at $25 per night with a two-night minimum stay. Seek reservations well in advance. P.O. Box 298, Koloa, HI 96756 (742-9921).

High in Koke'e State Park, Koke'e Lodge Cabins offer cabins to shelter you from the cool and rainy climate. $35 gets you a fully applianced, but rustic experience. Contact them at: P.O. Box 819, Waimea, HI 96796 (335-6061).

Kapa'a town is now the home of the new Kauai International Hostel. They offer $15 bunks as well as private rooms, some with a partially obscured ocean view in the best part of old Kapa'a. Contact them at: 4532 Lehua Street, Kapa'a, HI 96746 (1-800-858-2295).

Camping Supplies

Pedal and Paddle in the Ching Young Shopping Village in Hanalei carries a complete selection of the essentials, including gas canisters for stoves. In Lihue and Kapa'a there are a variety of huge discount stores along the Highway. On the west end, the tiny Hanapepe Hardware Store on the Hanapepe town loop road carries some supplies, including gas cartridges.

Groceries

Grocery stores are numerous and far flung. The only places remote from supplies are upland Koke'e Park, 16 miles above the Menehune Market in Waimea; Polihale State Park in the northwest frontier and 15 miles beyond the market in Waimea; and Ha'ena in the northeast extreme, 6.8 miles from Hanalei. Papaya's Natural Foods offers organic produce in Kapa'a in the Kauai Village Shopping Complex on the Highway.

Restaurants

Though Kauai has suffered from renewed "development" following Hurricane Iniki, the fast food explosion hasn't yet destroyed all of the quaint eateries on the island. Try any one of the Ono Burger stores in Kealia, Kapa'a, or Hanalei for cheap eats: the teriyaki-ginger tempe burgers are a vegetarian delight. Generally, Kapa'a and Hanalei both offer several good cheap eateries. They are both small places, frequented by actual residents, shop around.

Bicycle Rental and Repair

•Bicycles Kauai, 1379 Kuhio Highway, Kapa'a, HI 96746 (822-3315).
•Bicycle John's, Unit 6, 3215 Kuhio Highway, Lihue, HI 96766 (245-7579).
•Peddle and Paddle, P.O. Box 1413, Hanalei, HI 96714 (826-9069).
•Outfitters Kauai, P.O. Box 1149, Poipu, HI 96766 (742-9667).
•Sea Sport, 2827 Poipu Road, Koloa, HI 96356

Lihue—Polihale: Kauai West Side

Western Kauai offers two of the most enjoyable camping experiences in all of Hawaii at Salt Pond County Park and Polihale State Park. Both offer quiet days and star-filled nights. Polihale is wild and wave tossed, while Salt Pond is a calm enbayment. Along the way you can taste the charms of artsy Hanapepe, quiet Waimea with its surreal Shingon Mission, and finally 11 miles of undeveloped beach. Beyond the road to Poipu, the route is lined with sugarcane and punctuated with magnificent red-rock-walled canyons.

The 38-mile ride to the end of the west side Highway 50, begins in congested Lihue and ends at remote and majestically beautiful Polihale State Park. Beginning at the intersection of Highway 570 and Highway 56 in downtown Lihue, the first 12.6 miles feature an often-steeply rolling up and down climb up over the verdant Ha'upu (Hoary Head) Ridge. You pass through the Knudsen Gap at 700 feet above sea level. Until you pass through Kalaheo town 12 miles beyond Lihue, the roadway shoulder vacillates between generous and non-existent. To add insult to injury, traffic on this stretch of road is pretty heavy, especially near rush hour.

Beyond Kalaheo the road drops to near sea level and stays there to the end of the road. The shoulder also becomes far more hospitable. It seems the lighter the traffic becomes, the wider the road is. After coasting down into Hanapepe, the road rolls gently through fields of sugar cane. In Kekaha town the road follows the beach for a few glorious miles before heading back into cane fields. The following flat, straight stretch of road may present you with formidable headwinds if heading north, and wonderful tailwinds if riding south.

Thirty-three miles beyond Lihue the pavement ends and you begin the final 5 miles of dirt road. If it hasn't been raining hard these cane haul roads are pleasant to ride on wide tires. If it has been raining, the red earth becomes slick and nearly impassable on skinny tires. The road ends at Polihale State Park, where the western side of the Na Pali coast begins. Polihale offers camping along a wave-tossed beach with fantastic views of the knife-edged cliffs of the Na Pali receding into the distance to the north, and views of Ni'ihau to the west. Due to isolation from electric lights, the stars are so bright that the Milky Way looks almost solid. The perfect place for a starlit walk on a beautiful beach.

If you are just arriving at the airport in Lihue follow Ahukini Road (Highway 570) from the terminal. After 0.5 miles encounter the stop light and intersection with Kapule Road (Highway 51). Continue straight heading uphill. After 1.6 miles Highway 570 terminates as it intersects Highway 56. Turn left to begin this ride.

Miles from Lihue	*Miles from Polihale*
0.0	*38.2*

Intersection of Highway 56 and 560 in central Lihue. Begin left on Highway 56 East.

0.2
38.0
Groceries: Watch for Hardy Street *makai* (seaward). A *makai* turn here will lead you to a well-stocked Big Save Supermarket. In the same complex, in the circular part of the building to the right of the market, is the office for county camping permits. Or if you need State Park permits, continue on Hardy one block past the market to the big concrete cube building straight ahead.

0.3
37.9
Highway 56 East becomes Highway 50 East as you turn right.

0.9
37.3
Supplies: Junction with Highway 58 *makai* and a large mall with a K-Mart and a Sears for camping supplies.

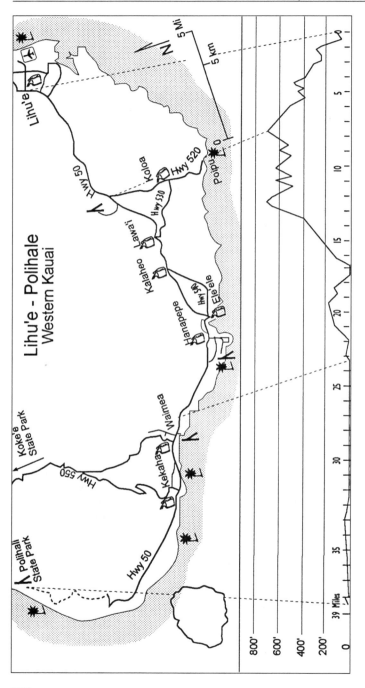

Lihu'e - Polihale
Western Kauai

3.6
34.6
Puhi town. Continue your roller coaster climb up to the ridge ahead.

7.0
31.2
Beach access: Junction with Highway 520 which glides 6.1 miles down to Poipu. The first 0.6 miles of Highway 520 rolls down through an otherworldly mahogany tree tunnel. Once-charming Koloa town lies 3.3 miles beyond Highway 50. Koloa has been reduced to a diversion for the mindlessly bored tourists stuck in Poipu with nothing to do. The Poipu resorts (there is no town) lies 2.8 miles beyond Koloa. From Koloa you can take Highway 530 west and rejoin Highway 50 in Lawa'i town. Highway 530 climbs 350 feet over 3.8 miles of shoulderless, cane-lined roadway.

7.4
30.8
Entrance to Kahili Mountain Park offering cabins starting at $25 per night. Follow the gravel road up the hill 1 mile.

7.9
30.3
Highest point on the route at 700 feet but the climbing and dipping are not yet finished.

10.1
28.1
Menehune Market with cool drinks and snacks.

10.8
27.4
Highway 530 (Koloa Road) leaves *makai* (seaward) to Poipu 6.2 miles below.

12.2
26.0
Intersection with Opu Road in Kalaheo town. There are various services available here including a grocery and several restaurants, as well as a pleasant coffee shop and bakery *makai* just beyond Opu Road.

12.6
25.6
Intersection with Highway 540 *makai*. Take a moment to enjoy the panorama of ocean and cane fields unfolding below you. Though Highway 540 may seem a good alternate route, it is shoulderless and it also misses a great view of Manuahi Valley.

175

13.9
24.3
That was your last gully, now glide 3 miles down to Hanapepe.

16.3
21.9
Ele'ele town with a Big Save Market and a Laundromat just beyond the intersection with Highway 541. Continue on Highway 50.

16.4
21.8
Scenic route: follow the signs *mauka* (inland) to old Hanapepe town featuring a few galleries and a few high-end restaurants. Watch for tiny Hanapepe Hardware store *makai* for gas cartridges for your stoves and lanterns.

17.1
21.1
On Highway 50 cross the Hanapepe River. There is a market just past the bridge.

17.4
20.8
Highway 543 *makai* (seaward turn) to Salt Pond County Park. To reach this pleasant camping area and one of the best swimming beaches on Kauai, follow the road 0.5 miles. Beyond the cemetery turn right following the signs to the Humane Society whose denizens will likely serenade you in the middle of the night. The Park begins 1.4 miles from the main Highway 50. There are open air showers, water, covered pavilions, and clean restrooms.

19.0
19.2
A small roadside market.

23.1
15.1
Watch carefully for the turn to Lucy Wright Beach Park *mauka* (inland) as you enter Waimea town. Lucy's place is an unremarkable campground too small and too close to town for its own good. Point of Interest: just past Lucy Wright Park Menehune Road leaves *mauka* to the highly over-rated Menehune Ditch. However, the Waimea Shingon Mission with its 100 Buddhas enshrined within strange bullet/phallus shaped stupas is worth the 0.6 mile trip down Waimea Road. Watch for Pule Road on the left and follow it 100 yards to the Mission.

Waimea is also the home of two supermarkets, both at road side in the center of Waimea town. The Big Save market is the last supermarket on the highway if you are going to the end of the road, or up Waimea Canyon Road.

23.7
14.5
Alternate route: Waimea Canyon Road leads *mauka*. See the Koke'e State Park Loop route for a description of Waimea Canyon Road.

25.8
12.4
The road swings close to the beach for a wonderful view of Ni'ihau island across the Kaulakahi channel. Ni'ihau is wholly owned by a *haole* family, but only native Hawaiians are allowed to live there.

26.8
11.4
Groceries: Junction with Highway 550 up to Koke'e State Park just past the sugar mill smoke-stack. The Menehune Road Market is at the intersection of Highway 550 and Kekaha Road 0.3 miles from Highway 50. This is the last market on this route.

Beyond Kekaha the prevailing wind becomes more squarely in your face. For the next 5 miles the flat, straight highway approaches the cliffs of Polihale in the distance.

33.0
5.2
Past the entrance to a military facility the highway branches, stay right.

33.5
4.7
A small green sign directs you Polihale seekers to turn left onto a earth road. However, if you continue on for 0.4 miles on the paved road, then turn left just past a "Truck Crossing" sign onto a second earthen road, you'll have a smoother ride.

35.0
3.2
Join the official road to Polihale, continue straight.

37.2
1.0
A rustic sign announces that you are entering Polihale Park.

38.2
0.0
Follow the signs and take a left up a short steep hill to a beach view and the beginning of the camping area which extends for 0.5 miles along the beach.

Waimea Canyon—Koke'e State Park

Of the three rides covered on Kauai, the ascent to Koke'e State Park is the most breathtaking, both in terms of how hard you must breathe to mount this height, and in terms of the views along the way. After the initial 7 1/2, miles which offer an increasingly expansive view of the coastline below and Niihau Island beyond, the route reaches the Canyon rim. Numerous viewpoints along the way offer views of the multi-head, 2,000-foot-deep Waimea Canyon. Waterfalls, red cliffs, and white rapids punctuate the extensive forests below while mountain air rushes off the summit above to cool you. The Koke'e Lodge and Museum offer a welcome break and often a warm fire. Beyond lie two views overlooking the wild Na Pali coast through magnificent gorges 4,000 feet below. The ride back down, needless to say, is a real hoot.

The 20-mile ride up to the end of the road at the Puu o Kila overlook is both demanding and rewarding. Though the first part of the ascent can be made on your choice of two roads, both aggressively climb to 2300 feet above sea level in just 6.5 miles. That is an average grade of nearly 7 percent. Waimea Canyon Drive meets Highway 50 just west of downtown Waimea. After a brief gentle climb the roadway slashes viciously up the first of several knee-bursting pitches, separated by flatter stretches and even a few downhills. The attractive thing about Waimea Canyon Drive is that it closely follows the rising edge of the chasm, which becomes the ineffably beautiful Waimea Canyon. However, because of the extremely steep pitches, I recommend that Waimea Canyon Drive be saved for your descent from the Park.

The more recently developed Highway 550 out of Kekaha town climbs to the same elevation in almost exactly the same distance, however it is graded much more evenly. It is, therefore, unrelenting. Highway 550 is also the preferred bus route so be prepared for some traffic and go early in the day if possible. Once the roadway clears a steep ravine it climbs over the exposed western shoulder of Kauai. Excellent views of the coast expand behind you as the island Ni'ihau comes more clearly into view. Whichever way you choose to climb, be prepared for a steep, shoulderless ride, and carry all the water you will need to reach Koke'e Lodge where the first reliable water stop awaits.

After the two roads join, the Highway climbs another 1,000 feet over the next 4 miles. The forest becomes richer and more moist as you approach the summit. There are numerous lookouts where you can rest your legs and lift your spirits. The further you go the deeper the canyon becomes. Distant waterfalls drape red cliffs adorned with lush forests, and beyond your toes you can see the special world created around the stream itself.

The campground and rental cabins cluster around the Koke'e Lodge and free museum. At 3,900 feet, it is often cool in these highlands and often very wet. Be aware of becoming too cool, especially on your descent. Hypothermia is very subtle and very possible when a sweating cyclist coasts downhill in a cool drizzle, even in Hawaii.

From the Lodge, it is only 3.7 miles to the end of the road and the spectacular lookout over the green cliffs of the Na Pali coast. The Puu o Kali Lookout is only 380 feet feet above the lodge, however the road see-saws tiringly over uneven terrain. Allow at least 30 minutes to complete the last 4 miles. Also beware of potholes at the bottom of downhill glides; runoff often courses over the roadway and erodes the pavement.

Miles from   *Miles from*
Kekaha   *Puu o Kali*
0.0   *20.4*

Begin at the intersection of Highways 50 and 550 on the beach in Kekaha town. Turn *mauka* (inland) on Highway 550.

0.2
20.2

The Menehune Market and bus loading zone. This is a fine place to stock up for your ride into Koke'e Park. Take on as much liquid as you will need to climb 4,000 feet over 16 miles. Continue along Highway 550 as it leaves town and skirts the base of the hill for 0.8 miles.

1.0
19.4

The road swings to the right as you enter a ravine and begin to ascend.

3.6
16.8

Climbing out of the valley, the highway makes a sweeping right turn as you break out onto the open shoulder of the island. You've climbed to 1,050 feet.

6.4
14.0

A wide spot in the road here is a great opportunity to stop and survey the coast below and Ni'ihau beyond.

7.5
12.9

Junction with Waimea Canyon Road at 2,350 feet. This is the recommended route back down to the coast.

9.5
10.9

The trail head for the Kukui trail down into the canyon below. There is also a short nature trail, a fantastically beautiful picnic area framed by white koa trees and good views. You're at 2,800 feet.

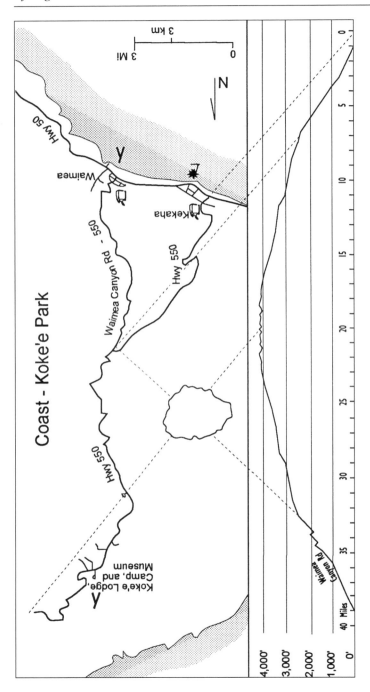

Coast - Koke'e Park

11.1

9.3

Overlook: Waimea Canyon Lookout is 0.2 miles up a steep little access road. The restrooms are often closed here and the water may not be running, but the view is never disappointing. At 3,100 feet now, the road grade becomes gentle after one final steep pitch, climbing only 400 feet over the next 3.6 miles.

14.9

5.5

Puu Hinahina Lookout. At 3,500 feet, this is one of the last grand views of the canyon. The restrooms will reopen when the State's budget crisis is solved.

15.4

5.0

Enter Koke'e State Park. The pavement gets noticeably worse here.

16.7

3.7

Koke'e Lodge and free museum. The lodge is a welcome amenity with hot food and a cozy fire. The museum is a real treasure for you natural history buffs, and the restrooms are blessedly open for those who need them. There is reliably available drinking water here. All of these facilities are clustered together at one end of a pretty meadow with inviting picnic tables. The campground is conveniently located at the other end of the meadow with its own rustic restrooms and indoor showers.

19.3

1.1

A short access road leads to the Kalalau Lookout at the bottom of a short hill. In clear weather you can look down into the isolated Honopu valley.

20.4

0.0

The last hill is steep enough to walk up, thankfully it is very short. Your reward is the Puu o Kila Overlook. The extensive Kalalau valley yawns beyond your toes as is stretches to meet the blue sea 4,200 feet below. The Pihea Trail begins here and continues into the highland of the interior. After just a few miles the trail encounters the Alakai swamp, an area of such intense rainfall and poor drainage that vegetation is limited to suprisingly low ground cover.

Alternate route

Alternate route

The description of Waimea Canyon Drive is presented from the top at Highway 550 down to its near sea level intersection with Highway 50.

0.0
6.8
Intersection of Waimea Canyon Road with Highway 550 at 2,350 feet. The junction is followed by 1.8 miles of radically steep ups and downs with precipitous drops into the canyon beyond the guard rail. Oh, and the views are outrageous. The roller coaster is followed by a brief level stretch.

2.0
4.8
You're at 1,500 feet

3.6
3.2
Another steep downhill as you zip below 1,000 feet.

5.3
1.5
The other side of that sign says 500 feet.

5.8
1.0
Start braking before you hit this turn. The pull-out on the other side of the road gives you a commanding view of the pretty settlement that is Waimea from an elevation of 260 feet. The next 0.4 miles brings you steeply into town.

6.2
0.6
Yahoo! Bottom of the steep hill. The local hospital is four blocks ahead just in case you don't make that last turn. That's so much fun it's tempting to turn around and do it again.

6.8
0.0
Waimea Canyon Road meets coastal Highway 50. An old sugar mill is just across the Highway and the Post Office is just to your left. Stores and services await just beyond the Post Office.

Lihue—Ha'ena: Kauai East Side

The eastern edge of Kauai is traced by Highway 56 which stretches 38 miles to road's end at Ke'e Beach and the beginning of the wonderful Kalalau foot trail along the Na Pali coast. Along the way there are three good campgrounds at Anahola, Anini, and Ha'ena; two delightful towns at Kapa'a and Hanalei; and 30 miles of bike-friendly road through scenery you'll not soon forget.

The first 7 miles are along a busy industrial highway with variable shoulders. As you leave Lihue you roll down to near-beach level and stay there until Kealia 10 miles away. Beyond the surfers at Kealia beach the broadly shouldered highway rolls up the eastern shoulder of Kauai for the next 19 miles, topping out at 440 feet above sea level. Along the way there are several opportunities to visit the beach, a lovely little river valley, and a waterfall.

Twenty-nine miles beyond Lihue you drop down to the lush plain of the Hanalei River crossed by the first of eight charming one-lane bridges. After the wonderful town of Hanalei (last chance for groceries) the highway swoops lazily along broad golden beaches and up over low headlands. Ha'ena State Park and Campground is about one mile from the end of the road, across from a cool wave-cut dry cave.

Finally the road ends at Ke'e Beach Park and parking lot. There will be no doubt in your mind as to whether you are the first person to ever walk on this beach, but the swimming is good, which is a little rare on this wave-tossed coast.

The swimming may be good, but the hiking is extraordinary. The 20-mile-long Kalalau Trail begins at road's end. It traverses up and down successive headlands and drops into valleys accessible only to hikers and boats. The trail beyond Hanakapi'ai Valley was closed in 1996, so check with the State Parks Department if you are interested in going beyond this first valley.

For the day tripper, the 5-mile roundtrip up and down into Hanakapi'ai makes for an unforgettable journey. The trail clings tenaciously to headland cliffs and you are never without a view as you travel through ever-changing micro-climates and vegetation. Bring water with you. The streams you'll encounter are not safe to drink from without first treating the water. In winter the shore at Hanakapi'ai is likely to be bouldery as the powerful winter surf carries away accumulated sand. More gentle summer surf may deposit sand. Always be wary of waves here.

If the periodically muddy trail to Hanakapi'ai beach didn't provide sufficient challenge for you, you can follow the stream up to a spectacular high falls with an inviting splash pool at its base, perfect for a cool dip. Though the trail to the foot of the falls is not long, it is perilous. Hawaiian mud is notoriously slick and there is no shortage of it along the way. The trail is also notorious for disappearing unexpectedly. You will likely have to ford the stream at least once. It's an adventure. Watch for abandoned taro fields and the ruins of a coffee mill along the way. Allow an hour up to the falls.

To begin your trip from the airport follow Highway 570 (Ahukini Road) 1.6 miles from the airport to its intersection with Highway 56 in the

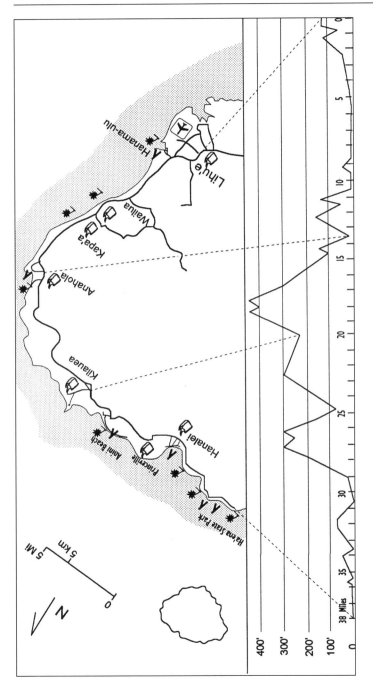

center of Lihue town. You can bypass the congestion and services offered in Lihue by turning right onto Highway 51 (Kapuli Road) at the first traffic light, 0.5 miles beyond the terminal. In 1.5 bike-friendly miles Highway 51 joins Highway 56 at route log mile 2.2 and you miss nearly 2 miles of unremarkable road.

Miles from	*Miles from*
Lihue	*Ke'e*
0.0	*38.0*

Begin at the intersection of Highways 570 and 56 in Lihue. Head northwest past a giant Walmart as the narrow busy road rolls up and down through town.

2.2
35.8

Intersection with Highway 51 to the airport. Stay left here as you enjoy a great view of the coast stretching ahead to razor edged Anahola Mountain on the horizon.

5.6
32.4

Point of interest: Junction with Highway 580 *mauka* (inland) with access to river boat rides, two *heiaus,* and the classic Kamokila Hawaiian Village Resort. This is also the beginning of Wailua, town which is slowly melding with Kapa'a in a flurry of beachfront condominiums. The Coconut Plantation Market Place *makai* offers shopping galore.

7.0
31.0

A giant Safeway and its associated strip mall welcomes you to Kapa'a. This is the last big grocery store until Princeville, 18 miles ahead.

Old Kapa'a begins soon after Safeway. There you will find a laundromat followed shortly by Bicycles Hawaii offering supplies and repairs. Across from the bike shop is an Ono Burger store and the marvelous Kapa'a Bagelry and Espresso shop featuring freshly baked goodies. Ignore the bike route signs in town. Most of them lead you into the gaping maws of several indigenous canines. The International Hostel is just beyond the bike shop and one block *mauka* on Lehua Street. As you leave town you pass the Full Belly Deli and Smoothie joint featuring its own ocean view outdoor dining area.

For the next 20 miles the shoulder is pretty generous and local traffic decreases radically.

9.9
28.1

Kealia surfing beach. Leave the beach here and climb a small hill before dropping back down into Anahola.

12.4
25.6
Beach access: Anahola Road. A coastward turn (*makai*) here brings you to Anahola County Park and Campground.

13.3
24.7
Anahola Road again. Turn *makai* to reach Anahola Park. This often windy campground is lovingly cared for by its resident custodian. It enjoys both a beautiful setting and access to a 3-mile-long beach custom made for long walks. Showers, water, and restrooms are available to all.

Anahola town is just beyond Anahola Road. It has a small market and a post office.

13.7
24.3
Side trip: Aliomanu Road *makai*. This serene two mile long dead end can only take you to heaven. Its a pointless, marvelous little side trip.

The highway rolls up and down as it climbs to its high points at 17.8 and 18.4 miles beyond Lihue at an elevation of 440 feet.

22.7
15.3
Side trip: Roll down into Kilauea town. A *makai* turn at the Menehuene Market starts you on a 1.7-mile side trip to the Kilauea lighthouse and a nearby albatross rookery. Both are frequently closed to the public. 0.5 miles along the way you can stop at Farmer's Market featuring deli food with an upscale pizza restaurant next door. Check out the lava stone church just one block off the Highway.

24.6
13.4
Stop at this overlook for a breathtaking view of the tranquil Kalihiwai valley-lined with gardens of taro, banana, guava, and other Hawaiian staples. There is a roadside waterfall just before the lookout.

25.2
12.8
Beach access: Kalihiwai Road. Turn *makai* for access to Anini Beach County Park and Campground and a beautifully quiet dead-end amble along 2.5 miles of beach. 0.2 miles from the Highway, turn left on Anini Road and drop steeply down to the beach. The Park stretches for nearly 0.5 miles with camping at the far end, 1.6 miles from the highway. This shady campground offers the usual restrooms and showers. The road continues on for another mile ending at a peaceful cove. Due to an extensive reef and shallow water, Anini is not especially good for swimming. It is an excellent place for reef walking and fishing.

27.9
10.1

After rolling up and down through several gullies you come to the Princeville Shopping Center with a well-stocked supermarket and several upscale restaurants. Beyond the shopping center, and within the planned community, are two fabulously expensive resort hotels with great views of the north coast below.

Just beyond Princeville, Highway 56 becomes Highway 560. Also there is a viewpoint overlooking the Hanalei River valley that simply melts my heart every time I see it. Taro fields in various stages of maturity and shades of green lead away to the feet of ridges that raise themselves up to the clouds as their humped spines become razor sharp, honed by the relentless rains.

29.0
9.0

Your first one lane bridge awaits at the bottom of a steep little hill.

30.6
7.4

Beach access: Aka Road marks the eastern edge of Hanalei. It also provides access to the weekends-only campground at Hanalei Beach County Park. The North Shore Bike Doctor is just beyond Aka Road.

The center of Hanalei lies 0.3 miles beyond Aka Road on the Highway. All services are clustered tightly together here. The Ching Young Shopping Center has some affordable eateries, a supermarket, a natural foods store, and Pedal and Paddle offering rackless rental bikes, repairs, and a basic selection of camping supplies (including gas cartridges). Across the Highway there are several more eateries, a coffee shop and bakery, and a pretty good happy hour. This is your last chance for groceries if continuing on.

Beyond Hanalei the Highway rolls gently along the coast over seven more one-lane bridges as you pass quiet rural homes, big beaches, and Charo's Restaurant and Nightclub. Cootchie, Cootchie.

37.6
0.4

Ha'ena Beach State Park and Campground with ocean-side camping, water, restrooms, and semi-private open air showers. This is a wonderful site for a campground, but like many State Parks in Hawaii, it seems a little tired. It is especially pleasant later in the day and early in the morning before the tourists return for their Na Pali adventure.

38.0
0.0

End of Highway 560 and the beginning of the parking lot. Ke'e beach is *makai* here of course. The trail head for the Kalalau foot path is well marked at the end of the parking lot.

From the Kalalau Trail at the end of Highway 560, the headlands of the Na Pali coast march into the distance framed by koa and ti trees.

Five miles above Waimea on the alternate descent route. Waimea Canyon Road is poorly graded and features several steep drops and climbs; it is tolerable if encountered riding down. The constant view into Waimea Canyon is unforgettable.

Chapter 7

Oahu

Oahu is only the third largest island in the chain, however, it is home for about 80 percent of all Hawaiian citizens. As you might expect, this condition has led to considerably more concentrated development than on the so-called outer islands. Honolulu itself contains nearly 750,000 people and, with the aid of three freeways, it spreads its tentacles ever farther around the island.

Fortunately, there are bicycle advocates on the island which have lobbied to improve bike access to various parts of the island. The State Department of Transportation has even produced a cycling guide map for the island. To get a free copy write to: State of Hawaii, Department of Transportation, Bicycle Pedestrian Coordinator, 869 Punchbowl, Honolulu HI 96813, (587-2160). As a result of these efforts, Honolulu is not the cyclists' nightmare that many major cities have become and you can safely, and even enjoyably, traverse the length of this busy city on certain designated routes.

The opening of Interstate Highway 3 adds a third shortcut route to the windward side of Oahu. Bicycles, however, are restricted to the two older Highways over the pali, and the Likelike Highway 63 is not recommended for bike traffic due to the length of the tunnel and the steep pitch encountered if traveling west toward Honolulu. The tunnels on the Pali Highway 61 are shorter and the grade more gentle. The approaches from both sides are also more bike-friendly than the industrial Likelike Highway. A description of the Pali Highway 61 is offered as a side trip in the Big Loop route log at mile 29.0.

There are two major routes covered in this chapter. The first, the Oahu Century, covers the 100 miles around the long eastern Ko'olau and Ko'olau Poko mountains as the road hugs the beach, and returns to Honolulu over the 1,000-foot high Wahiawa saddle. The second route along the Wai'anea Coast is presented as a one way spur. However, the intrepid among you willing to challenge four miles of unmaintained dirt road can easily make this ride into a loop complementing the Oahu Century, or it can stand on its own.

Traffic on Oahu is endemic. It is everywhere. On most of the coastal roads the maximum speed limit is 45 miles per hour and motorists are generally pretty good about observing it. But keep in mind that many drivers are tourists watching the sights as much as the road. Those scars in the concrete bridge walls aren't from skateboards.

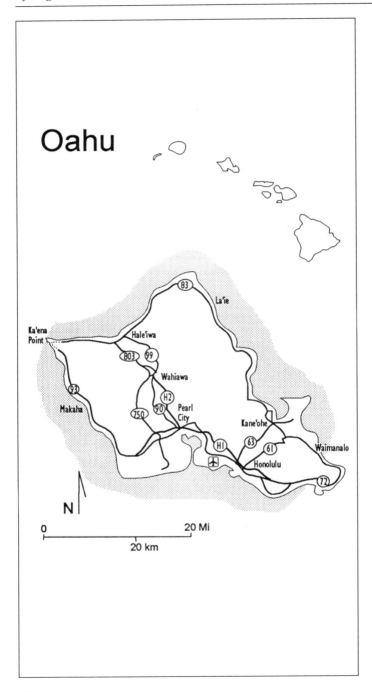

Amid the wide diversity of Pacific enthicities on Oahu is a large population of Native Hawaiians. You may notice that they usually aren't the ones driving the convertible BMWs. Like Native people around the world, most Hawaiians have been denied access to the wealth that *haoles* extract from their land. Understandably there is some bitterness. Of all the islands, you are more likely to personally experience this bitterness on Oahu. As a result, many *haoles* avoid camping on Oahu. One hears stories of slashed tents and such. There is an unusual abundance of broken automobile glass in the parks. I have never had a serious problem with native people on Oahu. Most people, if treated with respect, will reciprocate. Carefully avoid antagonism and your trip should go successfully.

Barring the use of the Pali highways, Oahu offers a marvelous 100-mile, coast-hugging, fairly flat loop. This route is described in the Oahu Century Route. The primary direction of travel is counter-clockwise. Certainly you can travel clockwise using this guide, however, traveling counter-clockwise has two benefits. First, you are always on the beach-side (*makai*) of the highway so the views are better and so is your access to them. Secondly, though the shoulders on the circumference Highways are generally adequate, if surveyors had to squeeze one side or the other, they more often squeezed the inland (*mauka*) side. The Oahu Century Route begins and ends at the Honolulu Airport.

Getting There

Not long ago, all flights led to Honolulu. This is slowly changing. Many airlines land first at Kahului, Maui on alternate days before proceeding on to Oahu. The only problem incumbent in this new scheme is that your flight will take about one hour longer. No plane change is necessary.

Perhaps the best part about flying to Honolulu is that it is still the cheapest ticket to Hawaii. Shop around before buying your ticket. Usually you can get a round-trip flight from Los Angeles or San Fransisco for around $300. Remember that there are also charter fights through Rich International and Pleasant Hawaiian as well as the spate of commercial airlines.

The Honolulu Airport is a busy sprawling place, but newly remodeled so that the domestic flights are now easily accessible from the international operations areas. The airport itself is well designed and easy to navigate through. It is also largely open air, so pack some warm-weather clothes to jump into.

An especially welcoming feature of the Airport is that it is serviced by a bike path which parallels the ground-level Nimitz Highway for several miles. The path in turn joins with other paths and bike lanes in both directions to start you on your way.

Names and Numbers

Visitor information is available at the Hawaii Visitors Bureau, 2270 Kalakaua Avenue, Honolulu 96815 (1-800-624-8678).

Information about Oahu's excellent and extensive bus system is available at 848-5555. Recently the system began to offer bus bike racks on some routes.

Recorded weather reports are available at 836-2102, 836-0121, and 836-0234.

911 gets you emergency dispatch. There is also a crisis information clearing house at 275-2000.

You can also find information on Bed and Breakfast accommodations throughout the island from B&B Pacific Hawaii, 19 Kai Nanai Place (262-6026). The local Honolulu Advertiser newspaper also contains extensive listings of vacation accommodations. Most west coast University libraries subscribe to this major regional paper.

Camping

Camping at State and County Parks on Oahu is free, and you must have permits. The route maps and logs in this section discuss the location and conditions at the many sites.

The City and County of Honolulu are one and the same. Together they administer eight campgrounds on the windward side, two sites on the north shore, and 4 campgrounds on the western Wai'anae coast. With the exception of the Ho'omaluhia Botanical Garden Campground, all Honolulu Campgrounds are closed from 8 A.M. Wednesday through 8 A.M. Friday. Permits are available at: Department of Parks and Recreation, 650 South King, Honolulu, HI 96817, (523-4525). Ho'omaluhia is open to camping on Wednesdays and issues its own permits at Ho'omaluhia Botanical Gardens, 45-680 Luluku Road, Kane'ohe HI, 96744-1855, (233-7323). Honolulu County permits will not be issued further than two weeks in advance, and on Saturday are only available in the satellite County Hall in the Ala Moana Mall (immediately on the alternate route through Waikiki). However, there is usually space available.

There are several other satellite county offices located around the island. Check the phone book for the one nearest you. Make sure to call to confirm that the office is still open, and that it is open on the day you are going to be there. Several offices have been closed, and some keep sporadic hours.

The State of Hawaii has turned over the operation of two of its parks to Honolulu County, but still maintain Malaekahana and Kahana Valley sites on the windward side, Sand Island Park near downtown Honolulu (open only on weekend nights), and Keaiwa Heiau Park high above Pearl Harbor. However, these remaining sites clearly reflect the State's lingering financial crisis and are at best tired. Get your permits up to one month in advance from: Department of State Parks, 1151 Punchbowl Street, # 310, Honolulu, HI, 96813 (587-0300). Do not expect a quick response from the understaffed office.

Both the city and state offices are on the same block in downtown Honolulu. See mile 5.1 on the Big Circle route log for a description and easy access.

There are also three privately operated campgrounds that never close, but may fill up. Friends of Malaekahana are a concessionaire operating within the Malaekahana State Park. They stay open all week, and promise hot showers (which weren't working on my last visit). Like its state run neighbor next door, the camping is dense under sheltering ironwoods, both camps are secure at night, you are less than a mile from the Polynesian Cultural Center known for their luaus and evening extravaganzas, and both share a beautiful sunrise crescent of beach. Contact them at: Friends of Malaekahana, P.O. Box 305, Laie, HI 96762 (293-1736). $6 a night.

YMCA Camp Erdman is sited near the western end of the highway on the north shore. This busy camp offers warm showers and a rocky beach for $6 a night. If there is a spot for you, they stay open all week. Contact them at: P.O. Box 657, Waialua, HI 96791 (637-4615). Some cabins are also available.

At 2,100 feet above sea level, Camp Timberline awaits the restless hill climbers among you. Hot water showers and a dirt field for $7 per night. Cabins are also available. Contact them at: Queen Emma Center, 224 Queen Emma Square, Honolulu, HI 96813 (672-5441).

Other Accommodations
There are 8 low-cost hostel-like alternatives on Oahu, all are in Honolulu:
•Driftwood Hotel, 1696 Ala Moana Blvd. (949-0061), $60 for an actual room.
•Hale Aloha AYH, 2417 Prince Edward Street (926-8313), $15 dorms, $35 doubles.
•Hawaiian Seaside Hostel, 419 Seaside Avenue (924-3306), $15 coed bunks.
•Honolulu International AYH, 2323A Seaview Avenue (946-0591), $13 dorm beds.
•Interclub Waikiki, 2413 Kuhio Avenue, (924-2636), $15 bunks.
•Polynesian Hostel, 174 Kapahulu Avenue within the Waikiki Grand Hotel, Room 1001, $15 bunks.
•Royal Grove Hotel, 151 Ulunui Avenue (923-7691), $45 for a single with a kitchenette.
•YMCA, 401 Atkinson Drive (941-3344), $30 for a single with shared bath, men only.

Camping Supplies
•The Bike Shop at 1149 South King Street, Honolulu, HI 96813 (596-0588) at mile 5.9 on the Big Loop route log offers an amazing selection of outdoor supplies. The Bike Shop also has stores in: Aiea, phone 487-3615; Hawaii Kai, 396-6342; and Kane'ohe, 235-8722 (Big Loop route mile 33.0).
•Oahu is also host to numerous discount stores such as Longs and K-Mart for supplies.

Groceries
With nearly one million residents on this medium-sized island, it's hard to get more than 10 miles away from a major grocery store. With some really poor planning it would be possible to get to Maku Ka'ena State Park without

supplies. Excluding that possibility, simply watch the route maps for the nearest grocery to your camp and you'll do fine. Store-bought food seems a little more expensive on Oahu than on the other islands, and there is a tremendous dearth of freshly baked foods.

Restaurants

Oahu hasn't escaped the fast food corporations, latest campaign to saturate the hinterlands with minignoshes. Fortunately, the wide ethnic diversity of Oahu's residents hasn't been completely drowned by the avalanche of french fries. There is a plethora of Chop Suey restaurants; Thai, Viet, and Ramen shops are also available. If you're outside of Waikiki, watch for places full of locals for a recommendation of consensus.

There are only three restaurants I would personally recommend in this sea of mediocrity. The first is Bueno Nalo Mexican on Highway 72, just north of Burrows Beach in Waimanalo. The secaond, in "Historic Hale'iwa," the Coffee Gallery comes closer to making a good espresso than any other place on Oahu; some vegetarian fare and fresh baked goodies for breakfast and desert. Third, in Waikiki, try Ruffage Natural Foods at 2443 Kuhio for organic light meals.

Bicycle Rental
- The Bike Shop, 1149 South King Street, Honolulu, HI 96813 (596-0588). The Bike Shop also offers rental services at shops in: Aiea, phone 487-3615; Hawaii Kai, 396-6342; and Kane'ohe, 235-8722. The Bike Shop has locations directly on the Oahu Century route in downtown Honolulu (route log mile 5.9) and in Kane'ohe (mile 33.0).
- Island Triathalon and Bike, 569 Kapahulu Ave., Honolulu, HI 96815 (732-7227).
- Blue Sky Rentals, 1920 Ala Moana, Honolulu, HI 96813 (947-0101).
- Fantasy Cycles, 66-134 Kamehameha Highway, Hale'iwa, HI 96712 (637-3221).
- VIP Car Rental, 2463 Kuhio Ave., Honolulu, HI 96815 (924-6500)

Bicycle Repair
- The Bike Shop, 1149 South King Street, Honolulu, HI 96813, (596-0588). The other Bike Shops on Oahu also offers repair services at stores in: Aiea, phone 487-3615; Hawaii Kai, 396-6342; and Kane'ohe, 235-8722.
- Island Triathalon and Bike (IT&B), 569 Kapahulu Ave., Honolulu, HI 96815, (732-7227). IT
- University Cyclery, 1728 Kapiolani Blvd., Honolulu, HI 96826, (944-9884).

The Oahu Century—Counter-Clockwise

Oahu has been much maligned as overdeveloped. I disagree with this sentiment and you probably will, too, after completing this 100-mile circuit around the island. This tour offers the big-city excitement of Honolulu with a fascinating beach-hugging alternate route. Beginning at the wild south end, there are numerous campgrounds and beyond Kane'ohe the highway is seldom more than 100 feet from the ocean for 40 miles. Along the east and north shores there are dramatic razor-backed ridges, marvelous forested trails to waterfalls, the Polynesian Cultural Center at La'ie, legendary north shore surfers, and an intriguing highway-escaping bike path. Beyond Hale'iwa there is a side trip to the quiet beaches at Makule'ia and sacred Ka'ena Point. At Hale'iwa the route turns south and you climb through thousands of acres of pineapple as you cross the central isthmus. The Dole Pineapple Packing Plant and Tasting Facility greets you at the top. Diamond Head and the sky-scrapers of Honolulu welcome you on the horizon to the south.

Starting at the Honolulu Airport, this route slinks through industrial, then commercial, Honolulu. Thirteen miles later you finally leave the metropolitan area and enter a decidedly more natural environment as you climb 240 feet up over Koko Head before returning to an alternately rocky and sandy coast. Another climb over 130-foot Makapu'u Head ushers you towards the ever-busier environs of Kailua and Kane'ohe, the other big town on the island. Between Honolulu and Kailua the Highway passes four campgrounds, all with restrooms, water, and showers. There is seldom a lack of basic amenities on Oahu.

Highway 72 climbs steeply up to 400 feet where it becomes Highway 61, the Pali Highway, which continues on to Honolulu. At the same point Highway 72/61 intersects with Highway 83, which is the principal route around the north side of the island. Kane'ohe offers a wide range of services including a Bike Shop store and a satellite city hall for camping permits.

Beyond Kane'ohe the highway settles back down to the coast and stays there for the next 35 miles. Along the way pass seven campgrounds and numerous other beach parks all with restrooms, water and showers. Markets are also plentiful here.

It would be easy to cruise through this entire flat stretch in a single morning, but it would also be a shame. There are several points of interest along this coast and some enjoyable camping. The Valley of the Temples just north of Kane'ohe has a splendid full-size reconstruction of the original Byodo-in Buddhist temple from Uji, Japan, set in a tranquil garden at the foot of the Pali cliffs. Kahana State Park and Kaliuwa'a (Sacred) Falls both offer short hikes into the tropical rain forest. Popular with tourists, the Polynesian Cultural Center in La'ie is a slightly pasturized attempt by the nearby Mormon University to introduce *haoles* to the various cultures of the Pacific. The evening show and luau may not be completely authentic, but it's quite a show all the same.

Beyond Kahuku the road swings to the south and soon you are on the North Shore, global surfing mecca. This elongate community has installed and landscaped a beautiful bike path that runs next to the Highway, but protects you from the narrow shoulders and rubber-necking motorist.

Old Hale'iwa awaits you at the west end of the vernacular north shore. From there you can cruise 7.5 miles along the ever-less tranquil

Mokule'ia beach to pavement's end. For the adventurous, a 4-mile-long coarse earthen road continues all the way around Ka'ena Point to the western Wai'anae coast. Read the description of this side trip before committing yourself to it.

From Hale'iwa there are two routes back toward Honolulu. Highway 99-90-99 is the more direct, better graded, and broader-shouldered way. It is also more heavily traveled, treeless, and a little boring. The alternate route, Highway 803-99-750, is longer and has narrow shoulders, but it is also shadier, greener, lower at its summit, and saves you from the congestion that bites your butt at Whitmore Village and doesn't let go until the far side of Honolulu.

Whichever way you choose to get to Waipahu area, the industrial-strength Farrington Highway alternates with several miles of bike path to bring you full circle, back to the Honolulu airport.

The route begins and ends on the bike path across the ground-level Nimitz Highway at Rodgers Street, which takes you 0.5 miles from and to the terminal.

Miles from Airport counter clock-wise	*Miles from Airport clock-wise*
0.0	*99.1*

On Rodgers Street from the terminal, cross to the bike path on the *mauka* (inland) side of the Nimitz Highway 92. You want to turn right on the path and head towards Honolulu to go counter-clock wise around the island.

1.8
97.3

The bike path ends in a tangle of asphalt. Make your way across the various roads to the *makai* (shoreward) side of the Dillingham Highway and continue on the shoulder. There is a Gas Pro store for fuel cartridges just ahead on your right.

2.3
96.8

Camping: Sand Island Access Road leads to the *makai*. 2.5 miles down this bike-lane-equipped industrial road awaits Sand Island State Park and Campground, a suprisingly nice spot considering its immediate environment. The campground is only open on weekends, features a locked gate to stop night traffic, and offers an incredible view of downtown Honolulu.

4.4
94.7

Just after crossing a canal, turn *mauka* on Smith Street for one block and enter downtown.

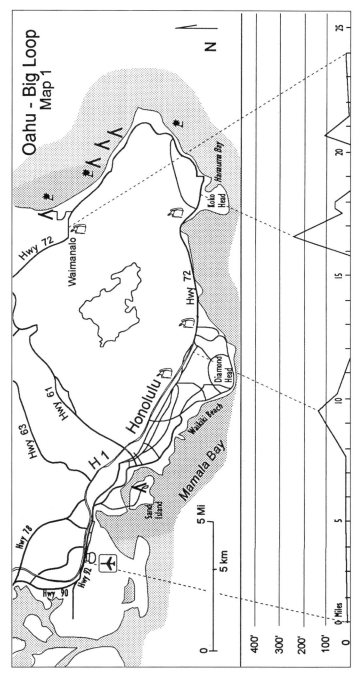

Oahu - Big Loop
Map 1

N

Hwy 72
Waimanalo
Hwy 72
Koko Head
Hanauma Bay
Hwy 61
Hwy 63
Honolulu
H 1
Diamond Head
Waikiki Beach
Hwy 78
Mamala Bay
Sand Island
Hwy 92
Hwy 90
5 Mi
5 km
0 Miles

0
100'
200'
300'
400'

0 5 10 15 20 25

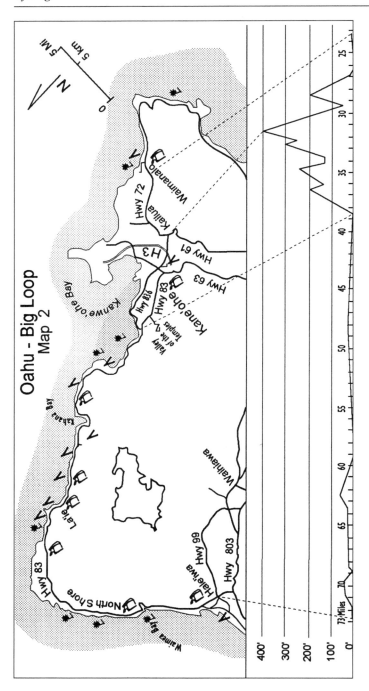

Oahu - Big Loop
Map 2

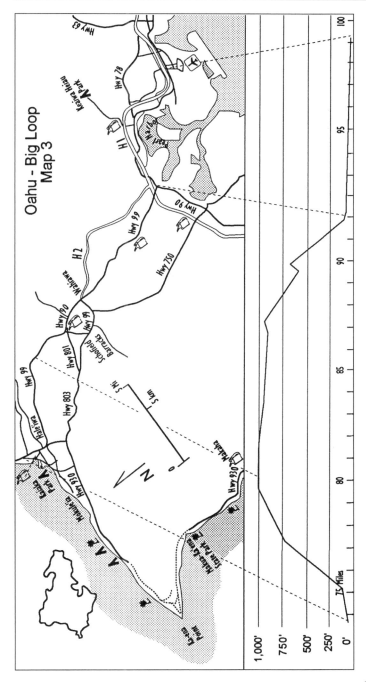

Alternate route

Alternative Route

Continue straight on Dillingham, which soon becomes Ala Moana Blvd., and takes you along the wharfs, through a park, into Waikiki, around Diamond Head, through a sleepy neighborhood, and back onto the Big Loop Route 9 miles away. This side trip is about 4.5 miles longer, and it's really interesting.

0.0
Smith Street and Dillingham.

1.6
Bike path begins and continues for .9 miles through Ala Moana Park *makai*.

2.5
Bike Path in the park ends. Get back on Ala Moana Blvd.

3.1
Turn right onto Kalakaua Street and roll into glamorous Waikiki.

4.5
The resorts end abruptly as you enter much-loved and used Kapiolani Park.

5.1
Turn right on Diamond Head Road and follow it around the point. Surfers, joggers, and fellow cyclists all love this area. See if you can spot Moloka'i on the horizon to the southeast across the Kaiwi Channel.

6.8
Continue straight on Kahala Road as Diamond Head Road peels off to the left. Continue on peaceful Kahala for 1.5 miles.

8.2

Follow the Bike Route signs left onto Keala'olu Avenue and continue on for 0.8 miles.

9.0
Cross busy Kalaniana'ole Highway 72, to the bike path on the other side and rejoin the Big Loop route log at mile 9.0.

4.5
94.6
Turn right onto King Street. The right-hand parking lane soon widens generously to accommodate bike traffic.

4.8
94.3
Alternate route connection: Bishop Street leads *mauka*. This is the western end of the Pali Highway through the central mountains. For a description, see Mile 29 on this route.

5.1
94.0
The very tall concrete building to your left is the city hall featuring the county camping permit office on the ground floor. Diagonally across the park area on this large block is the State Building at 1151 Punchbowl Avenue, which issues state camping permits out of office 310.

5.9
93.2
The Bike Shop is to your right. Need a bike, a sleeping bag, canned gas, a quick repair? These folks have just about everything a camper or cyclist could need.

7.4
91.7
Down to Earth Natural Foods and Deli on your right and a Star supermarket on your left. The roadway gets confusing here; follow the signs directing you to Harding Street.

9.2
89.9
Top of a steep little hill.

9.8
89.3
Turn left on 21st Avenue.

10.0
89.1
Turn right on Waialea Avenue and continue straight as the road becomes Kalaniana'ole Highway 72. The Keala'olu bike route joins the route here and a bike path is available on the left side of the highway for a while.

15.5
83.6
A big Foodland supermarket offers the last groceries until Waimanalo, 8 miles ahead. Begin the 0.8-mile, 240-foot vertical climb up over Koko Head and the legendary Hanauma Bay State Park and snorkeling thing.

16.9
82.2
A lookout point near the bottom of the hill provides an excellent view of this striking rocky coast.

18.1
81.0
Sandy Beach County Park and body surfing thing. Kauabunga, dude.
Restrooms and drinking water are available.

19.9
79.2
Begin a 0.5-mile 110-foot climb before dropping down to Makapu'u
County Beach Park and Campground. This is a pretty site, but not likely to
be serene so close to surfing and the Highway.

22.5
76.6
Waimanalo Beach County Park and Campground. Both this and nearby Waimanalo Bay County Park and Campground are sandwiched between
the Highway and the sea. Both have showers and restrooms and breathtaking views of the vertical cliffs of the Koolau Poko Mountains.

23.4
75.7
Waimanalo Bay County Park and Campground.

23.8
75.3
Bueno Nalo Mexican food. Yum. Mel's Market and some fast food are
just beyond in Waimanalo town.

24.7
74.4
Waimanalo Bay Recreation Area and Campground. This off-Highway
camping area was recently turned over to the county from the State, probably for financial reasons. This is a truly pleasant place to camp.

24.9
74.2
Makai turn to Bellows Beach County Park and Campground. This
large and lovely campground is off the road, security-gated at night, and
is only open Friday to Monday mornings. Permits are issued only at the
main office in Honolulu. If you're there at the right time, it is a very nice
place to camp.

26.5
72.6
Very gradually begin to climb up to the 400-foot-high intersection of
Highways 72, 61 to Honolulu, and 83 to points north.

Alternate route

Alternative route—Pali Highway to Honolulu

0.0
At 400-feet elevation, begin to ascend up the well-graded Pali Highway 61 from its intersection with Highway 83.

1.7
The grade eases as you enter the first tunnel at an elevation of 1,000 feet. If possible, wait for a break in traffic and rest before entering the tunnel. Turn on any lights you might have for visibility.

2.2
Emerge from the second tunnel at the top of this 1,160-foot pass.

3.0
Turnoff to the Pali Overlook. Don't miss this one.

3.5
On the far side of the highway, a segment of the Old Pali Highway dives off into the forest for a quiet ramble. It's worth the hassle of crossing the highway.

5.1
On the south side of the highway, the Old Pali Highway rejoins the busy road. If you are Kane'ohe-bound, do not pass this scenic little forest romp.

6.4
The relatively quiet Nu'uanu Avenue peels off to the right here and parallels the busy highway down to King Street-saving you nearly 2 miles of slightly hazardous riding.

6.8
A lookout over a fascinating Asian cemetery on the Honolulu-bound side of the road.

8.2
King Street in downtown Honolulu. You're at Mile 4.8 on the Big Loop route log.

30.9
68.2
Turn right onto Highway 83 and roll down into Kane'ohe town.

29.0
70.1
Turn right at this major traffic light-equipped intersection to continue on towards the north shore.

33.0
66.1
Camping: Just before a large intersection, Luluku Road leaves *mauka* and rolls 0.6 miles up to Ho'omaluhia County Botanical Gardens and Campground. This is an incredibly lovely setting at the foot of the Pali cliffs among plants and trees from all points of the Pacific. This campground is open on Thursday nights when all the other public parks are closed. Though it is part of the Honolulu system, you must obtain permits directly from the Gardens. Contact them at: 45-680 Luluku Road, Kane'ohe, HI 96744-1855 (233-7323).

33.2
65.9
Intersection with Highway 63/83 and Highway 836. At the southeast corner of this intersection is the Windward City Shopping Center with a good Thai restaurant, a big supermarket, and a Bike Shop with biking and camping supplies and repairs.

A major intersection and a choice. Highway 63/83 turns left here and skirts the northern part of Kane'ohe. It is busy with wide shoulders and takes you directly past the Valley of the Temples (see below).

Highway 836 is straight ahead here and is described in the alternate route that follows.

Alternate route

Alternate route—Highway 836

Highway 836 rolls through Kane'ohe past restaurants, a satellite City Hall, supermarkets, and the giant Windward Shopping Mall. Beyond town the shoulderless road drops down to the shore and stays there for a scenic 2.7 miles. A major intersection and a choice. Highway 63/83 turns left here and skirts the northern part of Kane'ohe. It is busy with wide shoulders and takes you directly past the Valley of the Temples (see below).

0.0
Intersection of Highways 63/83 and Highway 836. Stay straight on Highway 836.

1.0
A camping permit-issuing satellite City Hall at 46-024 Kamehameha Highway. It's a funky store-front next to a chop suey restaurant on the *mauka* side of the road next to the post office.

On the *makai* side of the street are two supermarkets.

Alternate route cont.

1.2

A *mauka* turn on Ha'iku Street will take you to Highway 83. Roll on down to the sea, but first cross a narrow bridge draped on both sides by mysterious hanging vines.

2.9

He'eia State Park and Fish Pond. For the next 2.7 miles swing in and out of quiet coves as razor-backed Mo'o Kapu o Haloa Ridge looms across the bay.

5.6

Rejoin Highway 83 at Mile 38.1 on the Big Loop route log.

33.2

65.9

Turn *mauka* on Highway 63/83.

33.7

65.4

Turn *makai* onto Kahekile Highway 83. Roll along the bike lane aside this straight, busy road.

36.3

62.8

The Valley of the Temples is *mauka* near the bottom of this short hill. For $2 you can visit a full-scale replica of a Buddhist temple complete with a 4-ton bronze bell that you can ring. There's a supermarket across the street.

38.1

61.0

Alternate route connection: Junction with Highway 836 and a small market.

43.5

55.6

Kualoa County Beach Park and Campground. This broad grassy expanse is far enough away from the highway to be quiet at night if your neighbors will cooperate. Showers, restrooms, and drinking water are available. The bay is really shallow here so swimming is difficult.

Over the next 14 miles there are numerous campgrounds and beach parks. All are equipped with restrooms, showers, and fresh water.

46.7

52.4

Swanzy County Beach Park and Campground. A narrow strip of grass between the sea and the highway with a small store across the way in a sleepy community.

48.4
50.7
Kahana State Park. Though the park reaches far up into the verdant valley and hills beyond the visitors center, the camping facilities are on a narrow, trash-laden stretch of forested land between the highway and a silty, trash-laden beach. The restrooms, 200 yards away, are 10 feet from the highway, and are in poor condition.

52.2
46.9
The busy trail head to "Sacred Falls," not a Native appellation. This 4-mile round trip hike begins in a banana plantation and enters a vegetative tunnel as it begins to gently climb into the hills. At trail's end is a pretty 40-foot falls with a refreshingly cool pool to swim in. This is a popular hike with the locals for good reason. It is beautiful.

53.3
45.8
Kau'ula Beach County Park. Another narrow grassy field across from a 7-11. And the night I spent here was restful and quiet. Camp near the ocean and it will drown out the road noise.

55.5
43.6
Polynesian Cultural Center in La'ie town.

56.2
42.9
La'ie Shopping Center with a really big grocery store. Ho'okilau Beach Park is 0.5 miles ahead.

57.4
41.7
Malaekahana State Beach Park. With a locking gate, it is secure at night, but theft from the parking lot during the day has become a problem. Well designed, off the Highway in an ironwood grove, and much used by the locals.

58.1
41.0
Friends of Malaekahana private campground. The management is disorganized, the showers aren't nearly as warm as advertised, and it will cost you $6 per night. And it is a quiet, secure, pleasant place to camp. Best of all, they're open seven nights a week. Contact them at: P.O. Box 305, La'ie, HI 96762 (293-1736).

58.8
40.3
Kahuku town with two markets and a bazaar.

63.7
35.4
A lovely little rocky beach park heralds your return to the beach you left back at Ho'okilau. North Beach begins here.

64.7
34.4
Watch for the beginning of the exquisite little North Beach Bike Path *makai*. There are several additional opportunities to join or leave this shady path.

66.0
33.1
Fabled Sunset Beach with surfers galore.

68.2
30.9
Watch for the Foodland supermarket across the Highway from Pupukea Beach Park, it's easy to miss.

68.4
30.7
The west end of the bike path as you roll down into Waimea Bay. The State Park up the valley is a lovely place, but the State is apparently trying to retire its debt through admission fees alone. Too bad. Waimea Beach Park is free. It has great sand and waves that will fill your shorts with sand all the way to the top.

72.7
26.4
Hale'iwa town: A right turn on Hale'iwa Street off the Highway leads you into euphemistically titled Historic Hale'iwa. The historic part has been paved over, I'm afraid, but there are stores, shops, restaurants, and The Coffee Gallery for pretty good coffee and baked goods. Don't let the unhappy barista harsh your mellow, just enjoy da java.

Kaiaka County Park and Campground is 1.6 miles beyond Highway 83 on Hale'iwa Road. The Park is locked at night from 6:45 P.M. until 7 A.M., and the camping area is in a wonderfully quiet seaside spot. The coast here is riddled with blow holes, very cool.

Side route

Side trip—Ka'ena Point and Highway 930

Beyond the intersection of Hale'iwa Road with Highway 83, there are three camp-grounds along the coast. Paved Highway 930 ends 7.6 miles beyond Highway 83. However, a rough earthen road continues two miles out to Ka'ena Point, where Hawaiians believed souls left the earth, where cane growers built a railroad, where pods of whales love to hang out, and where I once encountered two sisters, aged five and eight, cruising along on their pink sting ray bikes. The rough track turns south at the point and continues on two more miles to the end of the west coast Highway 930.

Along the way you will encounter slick mud if it has been raining, stretches of bone-jarring rocky road, and wonderful views of the beach and sea. 0.5 miles from Ka'ena point you will also encounter a gate especially designed to stop all motorized vehicles. You will have to carry your bike over said obstacle. Once around the point and heading south towards Makua -Ka'ena Beach Park, the best beach on Oahu, you will encounter a road washout. You will again have to carry your bike through this precipitous wash, and may even have to unpack. Beyond that, the Wai'anea Coast awaits you.

0.0

Intersection of Highway 83 with Hale'iwa Road, turn on to Hale'iwa Road here.

0.7

Stay right on Hale'iwa Road. Hale'iwa town is immediately to the left up the hill here.

1.6

Kaiaka Beach County Park and Campground. A serene, secure place to stay, nearly in town.

2.4

Turn right on Waialua Road.

2.8

Turn left following the signs to Waialua and Ka'ena.

3.7

Intersection with Farrington Highway 930. Turn right to continue on to Ka'ena and Mokule'ia District. Turn left to take the scenic route over the Waialua saddle.

7.5

Dillingham Airport, home of glider plane rides and sky diving adventures. The beaches along the coast here are lightly used and swimmable in low surf conditions. Delightful.

8.3

Mokule'ia Beach County Park and Campground. This grassy spot is well main-

Side route cont.

tained and heavily used by the locals, many of whom live next to the fence across the street. Full amenities.

10.4
Very busy YMCA Camp Erdman. See the chapter introduction for full information.

11.3
Pavement ends. The dirt and pointy stone track ahead leads 2 miles to Ka'ena Point.

12.8
Encounter a major barrier built to keep motorized traffic off the sensitive bird breeding grounds around the point. Heft your bike over the bars and ride on.

13.3
The track splits off in three directions. The upper track dead-ends at a nice viewpoint looking at Makua Bay to the south. The lower track heads out to the lighthouse on the point and soon runs into very soft, tire-grabbing sand, which is best walked. The middle track follows the old railroad grade as it cuts through a low hill and emerges 200 yards away on the west coast.

From the point where the two trails reconverge it is about 1.5 miles to the end of the Wai'anae Coast Highway 930/93.

14.8
Pavement slowly improves as you approach the beach and facilities at Makua-Ka'ena State Park. The intersection of Highways 90 and 99 in Wa'ipahu on the Big Loop route (Mile 83) is 28 miles to the south along the Farrington Highway (See Wai'anea Coast route log). End alternate route.

72.7
26.4
Intersection of Highway 83 and Hale'iwa Road. Continue straight on the Highway as you gradually begin the climb up to Wahiawa town 8.4 miles away beyond a 1,000-foot summit. If you need liquids or food, cruise through Hale'iwa and rejoin this route at Weed Circle above town.

74.6
24.5
Weed Circle above Hale'iwa. The main route turns onto Highway 99 here.

Alternate route

Alternate route—Highways 803, 99, 750 over Wahiawa Saddle.

To take the alternate, shady Highway 803 up the hill, stay right on Highway 83 for 1.4 miles.

0.0

Intersection with Highway 803. Turn left up the hill and begin to climb. The shoulders are very narrow, but the traffic is generally slow.

4.1

Just beyond the 900-foot summit pass the intersection with Highway 801 to congested downtown Wahiawa.

6.3

Intersection with Highway 99 at the bottom of a gully. Stay straight as Highway 803 becomes Highway 99.

6.9

ITC Bike Shop to your left.

7.6

Intersection with Highway 750. Turn right here. Roll up and down through shallow gullies and past various military installations for 4.6 miles, then begin a well-graded, 4.1-mile-long descent on a broad sunny shoulder.

16.3

End alternate route. Intersection with Highway 90. A left turn leads to Honolulu International Airport, eight miles to the south. A right turn to the west Wai'anea coast. The bottom of the hill is preceded by a large supermarket on the left.

74.6
24.5
From Weed Circle, begin the 4.4-mile, 1,000-foot ascent over the Wahiawa saddle on Highway 99.

79.0
20.1
Summit at 1,000 feet just before the Dole Pineapple Plantation processing plant and tourist center. Stop for a free cup of juice.

81.2
17.9
Turn left at the intersection with Highway 801/90.

83.0
16.1

At the intersection of Highways 90 and 99 continue down the hill on 90. The highway rolls violently up and down for the next 5.3 miles. This is a challenging stretch if you're north-bound. If south-bound up the hill, it's okay to walk occasionally.

88.3
10.8

The rolling stops and the downhill begins but is frustratingly interrupted by a series of traffic lights, often red.

90.6
8.5

Intersection with the Farrington Highway 90/7110. Turn left towards Honolulu.

92.0
7.1

Take a right on Lehua Street. Continue 0.3 miles and pass under the Freeway. Watch for the small green bike path signs on the left. This is the beginning of the 4-mile-long Pearl Harbor Bike Path which is pretty industrial at times, but at least it's off the Highway.

95.0
4.1

The bike path rejoins busy Farrington Highway briefly at Honomanu Street. You can reach Keaiwa Heiau State Park and Campground far above Pearl Harbor by crossing Farrington and following Honomanu Street for 0.2 miles. Turn right on Maunaloa Avenue and continue for 0.6 miles. At Aiea Heights Road turn *mauka* (left) and grunt and groan and grind the 2.6 miles up to the Park. This steep climb is rewarded by an additional 0.4-mile climb through the park to the camping area which is, like all State facilities, a little tired and often rainy. You are only 8 miles from the airport. Buy all the supplies you'll need at the bottom of the hill at one of the many stores.

96.2
2.9

The bike path becomes a bike lane on Farrington Highway at Arizona Street. The Arizona monument hovers in the harbor below.

97.0
2.1

Turn left up Radford Street. After 0.2 miles, watch for the beginning of the Nimitz Bike Path on the right and ride the path to the airport.

99.1

0.0

Turn right at Rodgers Street and cross the Nimitz Highway. The airport terminal awaits 0.5 miles ahead. You've just ridden around Oahu.

The Western Wai'anae Coast

The Wai'anae Coast is the closest thing to a desert you will find on Oahu, and guess where they've pushed the dispossessed natives? Generally this coast is overpopulated and under-resourced, and it shows. There are four campgrounds along the way, but except for Kea'au Beach Park, they are all backed by a four-lane highway and close to large towns with plenty of young folks with cars. The good news is that there are markets and restaurants galore. Services pretty much end in Makaha.

This route begins on the busy Farrington Highway from Honolulu at its intersection with Highway 99 down from the central plateau and Wahiawa. It is a 28-mile trip to the end of the pavement and the beginning of the 2-mile dirt track out to Ka'ena Point. Though reasonably flat, the volume of traffic and occasional narrow shoulder increases the fatigue factor considerably.

The first 12 miles begin with interminable strip malls and lots of cars. The 4 miles between Village Park and Kapolei begins with a short steep, shoulderless hill and continues as a flat, shoulderless, dusty, industrial access road. If it weren't in Hawaii, it would be ugly. The road widens near Kapolei, and you soon enter onto a four-lane highway which continues all the way to Makaha.

Beyond Makaha, the world changes. The road goes to a quiet two lanes with wide shoulders. Traffic slackens, the low income housing abruptly ends, and soon you are riding between a beautiful blue ocean shore and dramatic bowl shaped valleys with mountains as lovely as any on Oahu.

Makua-Ka'ena State Park awaits at pavement's end. The beach at Makua is my favorite beach on Oahu. It is nearly always sunny, there are good restrooms and showers to wash off the salt, the beach is wide, the mountains are lovely, and the ocean swells at the north end of the beach gently lull you up and down as you float in the warm azure waters. What a treat.

Miles from Pearl City	*Miles from Makua-Ka'ena*
0.0	*28.4*

Intersection of Farrington Highway 7110/93 and Highway 99. Follow the signs to Waipahu to the north.

2.7

25.7

Alternate route connection from Hale'iwa: Intersection with Kunia Road/ Highway 750 down from the central plateau. Stay straight and follow the signs to Makaha.

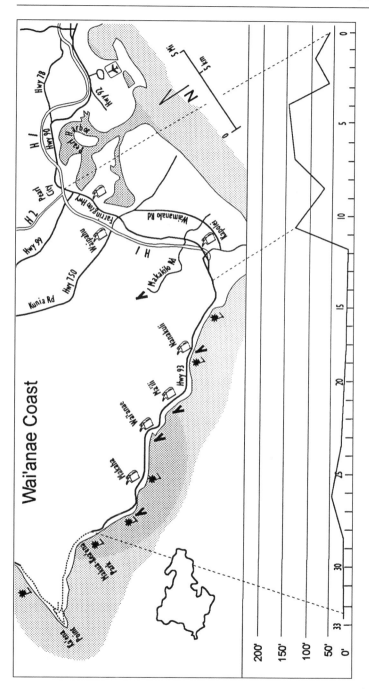

Wai'anae Coast

2.9
25.5
The Farrington Highway becomes a narrow two lanes and soon begins a steep, short little climb followed by 3 more miles of flat narrow roadway.

6.8
21.6
Enter Kapolei and a welcome bike lane. A new shopping center follows soon after.

If going to Camp Timberline watch for Makakilo Drive which intersects Highway 90 and climbs over 2,000 feet into the hills above you. Turn *mauka* onto Makakilo and climb for 2.7 miles. Turn left on Kikaha Street and at the next stop sign turn left again and proceed to the locked gate. You will need a four-digit code to get through the gate so make sure you have reservations before you climb the 2,100 feet up to the Camp.

8.0
19.6
Right turn on Kamokilo Road.

8.2
19.8
Right turn (*mauka*) on Kapolei Road.

8.4
20.0
Turn left after crossing Highway 3/93 and enter the highway on a generously wide shoulder.

11.8
16.6
Kahe Point Beach Park is the first Wai'anae coast campground. Across from the massive, roaring smokestack of the power generation plant the park has a nice view up the coast to the north. The beach is nice enough but the ambience is decidedly industrial.

13.7
14.7
Nanakuli County Beach Park and Campground. A high, earthen bank protects you from the Highway and lifeguards watch over you as you frolic in the very swimmable sea. Considering its location, this is a pleasant place to camp.

14.5
13.9
Supermarket and fast food.

19.1
9.3
Lualualei County Beach Park and Campground just beyond the Wai'anae Shopping Center and just before a large grocery store, the last supermarket on the coast.

21.3
7.1
Once-famous Makaha Beach, the ancestral home of longboard surfing.

23.7
4.7
Kea'au County Park and Campground. Though this is the largest campground on this coast, it is also the only beach park campground beyond the busy four-lane Highway 93, which becomes the sleepy two-lane Highway 930 after Makaha town. The coast is rough and swimming can be bruising, but there is plenty of sun and great views to the end of this undeveloped strip of Oahu.

26.0
2.4
Kane'ana Dry Cave *mauka*. Because the cave mouth points to the north, and the direction of the waves which cut the cave thousands of years ago, it's easy to roll right by this large orifice. You may also be distracted by the sight of a large squatter settlement that has grown along Makua Beach. These folks are almost exclusively Native Hawaiians who are determined to occupy this land. Though the State does not recognize their claims, nothing has been done to force the families to leave.

28.4
0.0
End of route. Makua-Ka'ena State Beach Park with glowing blue water against a golden beach backed by brilliant green-brown hills under a cloudless sky, ahhh. And there are restrooms, drinking water, and outdoor showers.

The road is navigable to passenger cars for another 0.8 miles. Beyond that you will encounter mostly hikers and bicycles over the next 2 miles out to Ka'ena Point. Hawaiians believed that when souls were through walking the earth, Ka'ena was their final departing point. Deserving souls left to the right and mean people took a left. See the Ka'ena Point side trip in the Big Loop route log for a complete description of this unpaved portion.

Mile 14 on the Ka'ena Point side trip. A cyclist cruises over the unmaintained Ka'ena Point road towards the gorgeous sandy beach at Makua-Ka'ena State Park. This is my favorite beach on Oahu.

Mile 64.7 of the Big Loop route. The quiet North Shore bike path gives you a chance to pull off the narrow highway and cruise through landscaped gardens.

Mile 3.5 and 5.1 on the alternate route over the Pali Highway to Honolulu. A two mile section of the old Pali Highway lets you escape from the freeway-like Pali Highway and instead wind your way through quiet, shady forests.

Just west of downtown Haleiwa at mile 72.7 on the Big Loop route. Quiet Kaiaka County Park invites you to a sunset just 28 miles from the Honolulu airport.

Mile 33 of the Big Loop route. Several small campsites are scattered throughout the Ho'o-maluhia Botanical Gardens perched above busy Kane'ohe at the foot of the pali cliffs.

Mile 36.3 of the Big Loop route. The Valley of the Temples, an operating cemetery, features an exact replica of the Byodo-in. It is well worth the $3 admission.

Mile 58.1 of the Big Loop route. Two miles beyond La'ie the Friends of Malaeka-hana private campground offers beach-side camping beneath feathery ironwood trees.

Bibliography

Description and travel:
Bendure, Glenda, and Friary, Ned. *Hawaii*. Lonely Planet, Oakland, CA, 1995. In the great tradition of Lonely Planet guide-books, this is a great low-cost guide to traveling (as opposed to touring) in Hawaii.

Best of Hawaii. Edited by Alain Gayot. Millan Gault, Los Angeles, 1995. A wittier-than-thou collection of reviews of Hawaiian amenities.

Bisignani, J. D. *Hawaii Handbook*. Moon, Chico, CA, 1995. Mr. Bisignani has written a series of current and comprehensive guides to all the islands available separately. Well researched and accessible.

Cagala, George. *Hawaii: A Camping Guide*. Hunter, Edison, NJ, 1995. A comprehensive review of camping facilities.

Gustafson, Sandra. *Cheap Eats in Hawaii*. Chronicle Books, San Fransisco, 1994. If cuisine is your passion, you'll enjoy this guide.

Let's Go: California and Hawaii. St. Martin's Press, New York, 1996. The quintessential budget travel guide.

McMahon, Richard. *Adventuring in Hawaii*. Sierra Club Books, San Fransisco, 1996. In case cycling has left you bored, here's some more stuff to do outdoors.

Pager, Sean. *Hawaii: Off the Beaten Path*. Globe Peqout Press, Old Saybrook, Conn, 1995. A guide to activities overlooked by the resort literature.

Tragaskis, Moana. *Hawaii*. Fodor's Travel Publications, Oakland, CA, 1994. A guide to the finer, high-price institutions on the islands a la Fodor's.

Pre-history and early post-contact:
Buduick, Rich. *Stolen Kingdom: An American Conspiracy*. Aloha Press, Honolulu, 1992. A culturally sensitive investigation into the politics of statehood and the dispossession of the Hawaiian people.

Daws, Gavan. *Holy man: Father Damien of Moloka'i*. University of Hawaii Press, Honolulu, 1995.

Kame'eleihiwa, Lilikala. *Native Lands and Foreign Desires*. Bishop Museum Press, Honolulu, 1992. The events leading up to and the effects of the 1848 *Mahele* in which the Hawaiian royalty agreed to authorize and recognize a system of land titling.

Kuykendahl and Day. *Hawaii: A History*. Prentice-Hall, Englewood Cliffs, New York, 1963. A good primer on the history of the Hawaiian islands.

Morgan, Thoedore. *Hawaii: A Century of Economic Change—1778 to 1876.* Harvard University Press, Cambridge, Mass., 1948. A fascinating study of the process of change from a moral economy to a cash economy.

Nakano, Jiro. *Kanda House: Biography of Shigefusu and Sue Kanda.* University of Hawaii Press, Honolulu, 1996. Insight into the lives of children in the boarding school system.

Stannard, David E.. *Before the Horror: The Population of Hawaii on the Eve of Western Contact.* Social Science Research Institute, University of Hawaii, Honolulu, 1989. A statistically inferred demographic study.

Summers, Catherine. *Moloka'i: A Site Survey.* Bishop Museum Press, Honolulu, 1971. Archaeological study of early inhabitants in the Halawa valley.

Native culture and history to present:

Bodley, John H. *Tribal Peoples and Development Issues.* Mayfield, 1962. A global discourse of the effects of colonization upon native peoples.

Bradley, Harold W. *American Frontier in Hawaii.* Stanford University Press, Stanford, CA, 1942.

Culliney, John L.. *Islands in a Far Sea.* Sierra Club Books, San Fransisco, CA, 1988.

Foltz, Tanice Gayle. *Kahuna Healer: Learning to See with Ki.* Garland, New York, 1994. A thoughtful exploration of traditional socio-cultural and herbal health institutions.

Ii, John Papa. *Fragments of Hawaiian History.* Bishop Museum Press, Honolulu, 1959.

Kirch, Patrick Victor. *Prehistory in a Windward Hawaiian Valley.* Bishop Museum Press, Honolulu, 1975.

Parker, Linda S. *Native American Estate.* University of Hawaii Press, Honolulu, 1989. Insights into the recent sovereign nation movement in Hawaii.

Shutz, Albert. *All about Hawaiian.* University of Hawaii Press, Honolulu, 1995. A complete English-Hawaiian, Hawaiian-English dictionary.

Natural history:

Edmondson, Charles H. *The Ecology of an Hawaiian Coral Reef.* Bishop Museum Press, Honolulu, 1928.

Hawaiian Biogeography; Evolution on a Hot Spot Archipelago. Edited by Wagner, W. L., and Funk, V. A. Smithsonian Press, Washington D.C., 1995. An exposition on the origin of island life.

Pratt, Douglas. *A Field Guide to the Birds of Hawaii and the Tropical Pacific.* Princeton University Press, Princton, NJ, 1987. An illustrated guide to the indigenous and introduced species of Hawaii and beyond.

Sanderson, Marie. *Prevailing Trade Winds: Weather and Climate in Hawaii.* University of Hawaii Press, Honolulu, 1993.

Stearns, Harold T. *Quaternary Shorelines in the Hawaiian Islands.* Bishop Museum Press, Honolulu, 1978.

Tomich, Quentin P. *Mammals in Hawaii.* Bishop Museum Press, Honolulu, 1969.

INDEX